A Collection of Timeless Recipes Inspired by Bobby Flay Chapter 1

A Journey through Signature Recipes, Culinary Inspirations, and the Art of flavor in Today's Kitchen

"A Collection of Timeless Recipes Inspired by Bobby Flay Chapter 1"

Table of Contents

1. Introduction: A Culinary Journey

The journey of culinary greatness is often marked by moments of passion, creativity, and a relentless pursuit of excellence. Few chefs embody these qualities as fully as Bobby Flay, whose name has become synonymous with modern American cuisine. His culinary journey began in the kitchens of New York City at the age of 17, and it has since taken him on a remarkable adventure that has transformed him into a global culinary icon. The world of flavor, for Bobby Flay, is not just about preparing food—it's about creating an experience that tells a story, celebrates diverse influences, and invites everyone to partake in the joy of great cooking.

Early Beginnings and Culinary Roots

Bobby Flay's story is one of a young man driven by a passion for food from an early age. Born and raised in New York City, Flay was introduced to a melting pot of culinary cultures that would later influence his cooking style. His initial exposure to professional kitchens came at the early age of 17 when he decided to leave his formal education behind to pursue a career in cooking. His first apprenticeship was at the prestigious French restaurant **Maison de Cuisine**, and from that point on, Bobby's drive and determination were evident.

During these early years, Bobby Flay honed the skills that would later form the foundation of his culinary empire—technical precision, an understanding of ingredients, and the ability to combine flavors in a way that would bring them to life. But it was his unique interpretation of American ingredients, and his innovative approach to Southwestern and regional American cuisine, that truly set him apart.

Flay didn't just follow the trends in the culinary world; he reshaped them. He recognized that flavor was at the heart of great food, and his constant exploration of flavor profiles became a central theme in his career. He didn't shy away from bold spices or vibrant herbs, and his use of chili peppers, smoked meats, and vibrant greens helped define his signature style.

The Global Influence of American Flavors

Bobby's ability to fuse the traditional with the innovative paved the way for what we now recognize as modern American cuisine. His culinary philosophy is built upon the belief that food should reflect both the culture and the ingredients of its environment. American cuisine, in his view, isn't just about hamburgers and fries; it's about celebrating regional diversity—from the seafood of New England to the southwestern spices and smoky barbecue flavors of the American South.

His career, which began in the kitchens of New York, soon expanded to the West Coast and beyond, earning him recognition for his groundbreaking restaurants like **Mesa Grill** and **Bar Americain**. Bobby's cooking reflects a desire to understand the roots of a dish while also pushing the boundaries of what food can be.

In his journey, Bobby Flay has not only embraced the flavors of his own country but has also drawn from his experiences with international cuisine. The influence of Mediterranean, Mexican, and French cuisine can be found in his cooking, but always with a twist that reflects his interpretation of the ingredients and the way they can combine to elevate a dish.

The goal of Bobby Flay's cuisine is to bring together a rich, diverse world of flavors in a way that is accessible, exciting, and unique. Flay's distinctive voice in the culinary world has had a significant impact on home cooking, bringing restaurant-quality dishes into kitchens across the world. His willingness to share his knowledge with home cooks, whether on television, through cookbooks, or in his restaurants, has inspired countless food lovers to elevate their culinary skills.

The Art of Flavor: Creating Memorable Dishes

At the heart of Bobby Flay's culinary philosophy is the art of flavor. For Bobby, cooking isn't just a technical skill—it's an art form that requires patience, intuition, and a deep understanding of how ingredients interact with one another. This section explores how Bobby Flay approaches flavor creation, from the importance of balance to his belief that cooking is an expression of self and culture.

The Importance of Balance

One of the most important aspects of creating memorable dishes is balance. When Bobby Flay speaks about flavor, he often refers to the delicate equilibrium between **sweet, salty, sour, bitter, and umami**—the five essential tastes that make up the flavor spectrum. Achieving harmony between these elements is key to crafting food that feels complete and satisfying.

For instance, a rich, smoky barbecue sauce might be balanced with a touch of sweetness from brown sugar, acidity from vinegar, and a dash of bitterness from charred herbs. These layers work together to create a dynamic and memorable flavor profile. Flay's ability to understand and manipulate these elements is what elevates his dishes from mere meals to unforgettable experiences.

The Layering of Flavors

In Bobby Flay's world, flavors are not just added—they are layered. One of the techniques he often employs in his cooking is **building flavors**. This can be achieved by cooking ingredients in stages, allowing each one to release its essence before another is added to create complexity. For example, when preparing a chili, Bobby might begin with searing meat to create a deep, caramelized crust, then deglaze the pan with spices and stock to create a rich base before adding fresh ingredients like tomatoes and chilies. Each layer contributes its own distinct character, but together they form a unified and flavorful whole.

Spices and Herbs as a Culinary Palette

Bobby Flay's love for bold spices and fresh herbs is central to his cooking. In many of his dishes, the flavors of **cumin, smoked paprika, chipotle, cilantro, and oregano** are brought to the forefront. These ingredients aren't just seasonings; they are integral to the overall experience of the dish. Flay's use of chili peppers, especially in his Southwestern-inspired dishes, creates an unmistakable depth of flavor.

By experimenting with these ingredients in different ways, he unlocks new and exciting tastes that capture the essence of American cuisine. The rich depth of flavor created by a well-blended spice rub or a zesty fresh herb garnish adds an element of surprise and excitement to every dish.

The Role of Cooking Techniques

The way food is prepared has a significant impact on the flavor. Bobby Flay often emphasizes that cooking techniques, from **grilling and roasting** to **searing and braising**, all contribute to how the final dish will taste. High-heat methods like grilling bring out the caramelization and smokiness in food, while slow-roasting allows for more delicate, nuanced flavors to develop.

Understanding the science behind heat and time in cooking enables Bobby Flay to bring out the best in every ingredient. Whether he's making a **perfectly charred steak** or slow-roasting a **rack of lamb**, each cooking method is chosen with care to highlight the natural flavors of the ingredients.

How to Use This Book in Your Own Kitchen

This book is not just a collection of recipes; it's an invitation to explore the art of flavor and discover how to create dishes that speak to your personal tastes. Bobby Flay's philosophy is rooted in the belief that cooking should be fun, creative, and accessible to all levels of home cooks.

Adapting to Your Taste and Ingredients

One of the main goals of this book is to give you the tools and confidence to **adapt each recipe to your own taste**. Flay encourages home cooks to experiment with flavors, whether it's adding a touch more chili for heat, swapping out a protein for one you prefer, or adjusting the level of sweetness in a dish. This flexibility is key to cooking with confidence.

Additionally, the book emphasizes the importance of **using fresh, seasonal ingredients**. While Bobby Flay's recipes are rooted in American flavors, he encourages cooks to think beyond the boundaries of any single culinary tradition. For instance, a southwestern dish can easily incorporate ingredients like **avocados**, **squash blossoms**, or **rosemary** based on what is available at your local market. By exploring different combinations of ingredients and techniques, you will develop your own signature cooking style.

Perfecting Your Technique

The book also focuses on refining essential cooking techniques—whether it's learning how to perfectly **sear a steak**, **make a smooth hollandaise sauce**, or **grill vegetables**. Each recipe comes with detailed instructions on these techniques, so you can build your cooking skills and take your dishes to the next level.

Building a Flavorful Kitchen

Another key aspect of using this book is learning how to build a **flavorful kitchen**. Bobby Flay believes that a well-stocked pantry is a critical component to making dishes come to life. This section will guide you in stocking your kitchen with key ingredients, from **spices and herbs** to **vinegars** and **oils**, so you are always ready to create a dish that bursts with flavor.

2. Foundations of Flavor: Essential Ingredients and Techniques

Building a Chef's Pantry: Key Spices, Herbs, and Ingredients

A well-stocked pantry is the foundation of any great kitchen. When it comes to building your chef's pantry, it's essential to focus on quality, versatility, and freshness. Bobby Flay's pantry is not just a collection of random ingredients, but a carefully curated selection of items that allow him to create deep, dynamic flavors and elevate simple dishes into culinary masterpieces. Understanding what to stock in your pantry is just as crucial as knowing how to use those ingredients.

1. The Essential Spices and Herbs

Spices and herbs are the building blocks of flavor. They bring complexity, depth, and vibrancy to your dishes. They're essential for crafting the bold, layered flavors that Bobby Flay is known for. Whether it's a fragrant **curry powder**, the earthy depth of **cumin**, or the bright zest of **cilantro**, knowing how and when to use these flavor boosters can elevate even the simplest ingredients.

- **Cumin**: A key spice in many of Bobby Flay's Southwestern and Mediterranean dishes. It has a warm, earthy, slightly smoky flavor. Cumin can be used in spice rubs, stews, curries, and roasted vegetables. The spice pairs beautifully with **chili powder**, **coriander**, and **garlic**.

- **Paprika**: A versatile spice that brings color and a smoky undertone to dishes. Smoked paprika, in particular, gives a deep, charred flavor that works well in **grilled meats**, **stews**, and **sauces**.

- **Chili Powder**: Used extensively in Bobby's **Tex-Mex** and **Southwestern** dishes, chili powder brings heat and complexity. It's essential for creating balanced spice blends for everything from **chili** to **barbecue rubs**.

- **Coriander**: The seeds of the cilantro plant, coriander has a warm, citrusy flavor with a slight nuttiness. It's a fundamental spice in curry blends, **Indian** and **Middle Eastern** cooking, and works well in **salsas**, **pickles**, and **stews**.

- **Turmeric**: Known for its bright yellow color and health benefits, turmeric brings a mild, earthy bitterness. It's often used in **Indian** curries and can be added to **rice**, **soups**, and **smoothies** for an extra depth of flavor.

- **Cayenne Pepper**: A fiery, spicy element that enhances heat in dishes. A pinch of cayenne pepper can transform a **salsa**, **soup**, or **rub** into a vibrant, spicy creation.

- **Thyme**: A herb that is part of many culinary traditions, thyme has a subtle, earthy flavor. It's great in **roasts**, **stews**, and **braised meats**. Flay uses thyme in **sauces**, **potatoes**, and **roasted vegetables**.

- **Oregano**: A key herb in **Mediterranean** and **Italian** cooking, oregano has a robust, slightly bitter flavor. It's ideal in **tomato-based dishes**, **grilled meats**, and **salads**.

- **Basil**: With its sweet, peppery taste, basil is essential in **Italian** dishes like **pasta**, **pizza**, and **pesto**. Fresh basil is also great when added to **salads** and **sauces**.

- **Rosemary**: This herb offers a pine-like aroma and flavor. It's perfect for **roasting meats**, **grilling vegetables**, and flavoring **potatoes**. Rosemary is also great in **bread doughs** and **cooking oils**.

- **Cilantro**: Fresh cilantro offers a bright, citrusy flavor that balances heavier, spicy elements. It's often used in **salsas**, **guacamole**, **curries**, and as a garnish for a variety of dishes.

2. Pantry Staples: Oils, Vinegars, and Condiments

Besides spices and herbs, there are several pantry staples that should never be overlooked. These ingredients are versatile and can be used in countless dishes, from **sauces** to **dressings** to **marinades**.

- **Extra Virgin Olive Oil**: Olive oil is at the heart of Mediterranean cooking, but it's also crucial in **American** cuisine. It's ideal for **sautéing**, **dressing salads**, and making **pasta sauces**. Always choose high-quality, cold-pressed extra virgin olive oil for the best flavor.

- **Canola or Vegetable Oil**: These oils are ideal for **deep frying**, **searing**, or **pan-frying** due to their high smoke points.

- **Balsamic Vinegar**: Known for its rich, tangy flavor, balsamic vinegar is used in **dressings**, **sauces**, and **glazes**. Flay often uses balsamic to create reductions or drizzle over **grilled vegetables**.

- **Apple Cider Vinegar**: This tangy vinegar is popular in **salad dressings**, **pickles**, and **marinades**. It has a milder acidity compared to other vinegars and can even be used in **soups**.

- **Soy Sauce**: A key ingredient in **Asian cuisine**, soy sauce brings salty, umami flavors to marinades, stir-fries, and dipping sauces. Bobby Flay often uses it to enhance **sauces** for **meat dishes** and **sushi**.

- **Hot Sauce**: For an added kick, hot sauces like **Tabasco**, **Sriracha**, and **Cholula** are versatile ingredients. They can be drizzled over **tacos**, added to **soups**, or stirred into **sauces** for heat.

3. Key Grains, Legumes, and Nuts

No pantry is complete without a selection of grains, legumes, and nuts. These ingredients provide both substance and texture to Bobby Flay's meals, from hearty **risottos** to savory **salads**.

- **Rice**: Both white and brown rice are essential, but Bobby Flay loves **wild rice**, which adds a nutty flavor and chewy texture. **Saffron rice** or **biryani rice** can elevate your dinner to new heights.

- **Quinoa**: Known for its protein-rich properties, quinoa is a popular base for salads, bowls, and as a side dish. It's a great alternative to rice or couscous.

- **Chickpeas**: Whether roasted, pureed into **hummus**, or added to stews, chickpeas are a hearty and nutritious legume. Flay often uses them in **Middle Eastern** dishes and Mediterranean-inspired bowls.

- **Lentils**: A quick-cooking legume that is packed with protein. Flay uses lentils in **curries**, **soups**, and **salads** for an earthy flavor.

- **Almonds**: Chopped, slivered, or whole, almonds are perfect for **granola**, **salads**, or even **desserts**. Flay uses them in **spice rubs** for meats or as a garnish for **vegetable dishes**.

4. Sweeteners and Flavor Enhancers

For a sweet touch or extra layer of depth, it's essential to have a variety of sweeteners and flavor enhancers. These ingredients can help balance acidity or add a little indulgence to savory and sweet dishes alike.

- **Honey**: A natural sweetener that pairs beautifully with **mustard**, **vinegar**, and **citrus**. Bobby Flay often uses honey to balance spiced **salsas**, **barbecue sauces**, and in **glazes** for meats.

- **Maple Syrup**: A rich, robust sweetener often used in **desserts** like **pecan pie** and **glazes** for roasted vegetables, **squash**, or even **brussels sprouts**.

- **Brown Sugar**: With its molasses content, brown sugar adds a deep, caramelized sweetness. It's key in **barbecue sauces**, **marinades**, and **spice rubs**.

A well-stocked pantry is just the first step in creating memorable meals. The next step is having the right kitchen tools to prepare those dishes. Bobby Flay's kitchen is filled with high-quality, durable tools that support both precision and creativity. Each tool plays a role in bringing out the full potential of your ingredients, whether you're preparing a delicate sauce or grilling the perfect steak.

1. Knives and Cutting Boards

Knives are the foundation of every kitchen. Bobby Flay's professional kitchen is stocked with **chef's knives**, **paring knives**, **serrated knives**, and **boning knives**, each suited for a specific purpose.

- **Chef's Knife**: This versatile knife is used for most tasks, including chopping vegetables, slicing meats, and mincing herbs.

- **Paring Knife**: A small knife used for precise work, such as peeling fruits or trimming vegetables.

- **Serrated Knife**: Essential for cutting through foods with a tough exterior and soft interior, such as **bread**, **tomatoes**, or **cakes**.

- **Cutting Boards**: Having multiple cutting boards in your kitchen is essential to avoid cross-contamination. Bobby Flay uses **wooden boards** for vegetables and **plastic boards** for meat.

2. Cookware and Bakeware

Good cookware is critical for both precision and consistency in cooking. From **heavy-duty cast-iron skillets** to **nonstick pans**, having the right pieces will help you achieve perfect results.

- **Cast Iron Skillet**: Known for its heat retention and even cooking, cast iron is Bobby Flay's go-to for **steaks**, **fajitas**, **cornbread**, and **sautéed vegetables**.

- **Nonstick Skillet**: Perfect for cooking delicate dishes like **eggs**, **pancakes**, or **fish** that need to be turned gently.

- **Dutch Oven**: Essential for **braising**, **slow-cooking**, and making soups or stews. Flay's Dutch oven is a staple for cooking dishes like **beef bourguignon** and **chicken tagine**.

- **Sheet Pans**: Ideal for **roasting vegetables**, **baking cookies**, and even making **pizzas**. Flay uses sheet pans for everything from **roasted potatoes** to **oven-baked fish**.

3. Small Appliances and Gadgets

In addition to traditional cookware, small appliances and kitchen gadgets are essential for streamlining tasks and creating more consistent results.

- **Food Processor**: Perfect for chopping, slicing, and pureeing ingredients quickly. Bobby Flay uses a food processor for making **salsas**, **hummus**, and **pesto**.

- **Blender**: Ideal for smoothies, **soups**, and making sauces like **tomato sauce** or **creamy salad dressings**.

- **Immersion Blender**: A versatile tool for quickly blending soups or emulsifying sauces.

- **Grill Pan**: For achieving those perfect grill marks and smoky flavors indoors when it's too cold or rainy to grill outside.

Techniques for Elevating Flavor: Searing, Braising, Roasting, and More

Cooking techniques are as important as the ingredients themselves. The **art of cooking** lies in the ability to elevate raw ingredients to their highest potential. Bobby Flay has mastered techniques that are central to achieving deep, layered flavors in every dish.

1. Searing: Creating Flavor Through Caramelization

Searing is a technique that involves cooking the surface of meat, fish, or vegetables at high heat, creating a flavorful crust. This caramelization enhances the natural flavors of the ingredients and locks in moisture.

- **Meat**: To sear meat, heat a heavy pan (like a **cast-iron skillet**) until it's smoking hot. Add oil with a high smoke point, such as **canola oil**, and sear the meat for a few minutes on each side, until a golden brown crust forms.

- **Vegetables**: You can also sear vegetables to develop a rich flavor. **Mushrooms**, **onions**, and **bell peppers** take on a smoky, caramelized flavor when seared properly.

2. Braising: Tenderizing Tough Cuts

Braising is a cooking method that involves cooking meat in a liquid at a low temperature for an extended period of time. It's perfect for tough cuts of meat like **brisket, short ribs**, or **lamb shanks**.

- **Braising** involves first searing the meat to develop flavor, then simmering it in a liquid (such as **stock, citrus**, or **beer**) until tender. The slow cooking process breaks down connective tissues and infuses the meat with the flavors of the cooking liquid.

3. Roasting: Intensifying Flavors Through Heat

Roasting involves cooking ingredients in an oven with dry heat, typically at higher temperatures. This method enhances the natural sugars in vegetables and proteins, developing complex flavors.

- **Roasting Vegetables**: Roasting brings out the sweetness in vegetables like **carrots**, **sweet potatoes**, and **brussels sprouts**. The high heat caramelizes the exterior while keeping the interior tender.

- **Roasting Meats**: For **roasts** like **beef tenderloin** or **chicken**, roasting at a high temperature initially helps develop a flavorful crust, and then lowering the temperature allows the meat to cook evenly without drying out.

Conclusion

In this chapter, we've explored the foundation of Bobby Flay's culinary journey, focusing on essential ingredients, tools, and techniques that make his cooking distinctive. Building your chef's pantry with the right spices, oils, and condiments will open the door to creating bold, dynamic flavors in your kitchen. Equally important are the tools you choose and the techniques you master, as they allow you to unlock the full potential of your ingredients. Whether it's searing a steak to perfection or slowly braising a rich stew, these foundational elements of cooking are the key to transforming everyday meals into extraordinary culinary experiences.

3. Appetizers and Small Plates: 25 Recipes

The Story of Flavorful Beginnings: Crafting First Impressions

The first impression is everything — and when it comes to food, appetizers are the first step in creating a memorable dining experience. Whether you're hosting a gathering or preparing a casual dinner for family, appetizers set the tone for the meal to come. For Bobby Flay, appetizers are an opportunity to showcase bold, vibrant flavors that awaken the taste buds and offer a sense of anticipation for what's next. From smoky, charred proteins to crisp, fresh vegetables, each appetizer tells a story of innovation and culinary mastery. This collection of small plates is inspired by the essence of Bobby Flay's creative spirit — dishes that blend tradition with modern flair, using fresh ingredients, expert technique, and, of course, an abundance of flavor.

Recipes

1. King Crab Gumbo with Crab Rice and Crispy Okra

Introduction: Bobby Flay's King Crab Gumbo is a refined take on a Southern classic. It combines the rich, smoky flavors of a traditional gumbo with the sweetness of **king crab** and a satisfying crunch from **crispy okra**. The crab rice adds an extra layer of flavor, creating a dish that feels both luxurious and comforting. Perfect for special occasions or a sophisticated starter, this dish captures the heart of Louisiana's culinary traditions while adding Bobby's signature twist.

Ingredients:

- 1 lb fresh King crab legs (or 2 cups of crab meat)
- 1 tablespoon olive oil
- 1 medium onion, diced
- 1 bell pepper, diced
- 2 celery stalks, diced
- 2 cloves garlic, minced
- 4 cups seafood stock

- 1 cup crushed tomatoes

- 1 tablespoon Cajun seasoning

- 1 teaspoon smoked paprika

- 2 bay leaves

- 1 teaspoon thyme

- Salt and pepper, to taste

- ½ cup okra, sliced

- 2 tablespoons cornmeal

- 1 cup cooked white rice

- 1 tablespoon fresh parsley, chopped

For Crab Rice:

- 1 tablespoon butter

- ½ cup onion, finely chopped

- 1 cup cooked rice

- ½ cup cooked crab meat (preferably from the King crab)

- Salt and pepper, to taste

Method:

1. **Prepare Crab Rice:** Melt butter in a skillet over medium heat. Add the chopped onion and cook until soft, about 3 minutes. Stir in the cooked rice and crab meat. Season with salt and pepper. Set aside.

2. **Make the Gumbo:** In a large pot, heat olive oil over medium heat. Add the onion, bell pepper, celery, and garlic, and sauté until softened, about 5 minutes. Stir in Cajun seasoning, smoked paprika, thyme, and bay leaves. Cook for another minute. Add the seafood stock and crushed tomatoes, bring to a boil, then reduce the heat and simmer for 20 minutes.

3. **Fry the Okra:** In a small skillet, heat oil over medium-high heat. Toss the sliced okra in cornmeal and fry until crispy, about 3-4 minutes. Drain on paper towels and season with salt.

4. **Serve:** Spoon a portion of crab rice into each bowl. Ladle the gumbo over the rice, then garnish with crispy okra and fresh parsley.

2. Charred Spanish Octopus with Smoked Paprika

Introduction: Charred **octopus** brings a bold, smoky flavor that pairs beautifully with the rich depth of **smoked paprika**. This Mediterranean-inspired appetizer offers a stunning presentation and a complex flavor profile. The natural sweetness of the octopus is enhanced by the smoky char and the earthy, slightly spicy paprika, making this dish perfect for seafood lovers and adventurous eaters alike.

Ingredients:

- 2 octopus tentacles (fresh or thawed)
- 1 tablespoon olive oil
- 2 cloves garlic, minced
- 1 teaspoon smoked paprika
- ½ teaspoon chili flakes
- Salt and pepper, to taste
- Fresh lemon wedges, for serving
- Fresh parsley, chopped, for garnish

Method:

1. **Boil the Octopus:** In a large pot of salted water, bring to a boil. Add the octopus and simmer for about 45 minutes until tender. Remove and allow to cool slightly.

2. **Grill the Octopus:** Preheat the grill to medium-high heat. Brush the octopus with olive oil and season with smoked paprika, chili flakes, salt, and pepper. Grill for 2-3 minutes per side until charred and crispy.

3. **Serve:** Plate the octopus and drizzle with additional olive oil. Garnish with fresh parsley and lemon wedges.

3. Grilled Shrimp with Mango Salsa

Introduction: The **smoky, charred shrimp** paired with a **sweet and tangy mango salsa** creates an irresistible appetizer. This dish blends the heat from the grill with the freshness of tropical fruit, delivering a perfect balance of flavor that is both light and satisfying.

Ingredients:

- 12 large shrimp, peeled and deveined
- 1 tablespoon olive oil
- Salt and pepper, to taste
- 1 mango, peeled and diced
- ½ red onion, finely chopped
- 1 small red chili, minced
- 1 tablespoon fresh cilantro, chopped
- Juice of 1 lime

Method:

1. **Grill the Shrimp:** Preheat the grill to medium-high heat. Toss the shrimp in olive oil and season with salt and pepper. Grill for 2-3 minutes per side until pink and slightly charred.

2. **Prepare Mango Salsa:** In a bowl, combine the diced mango, red onion, red chili, cilantro, and lime juice. Stir to combine and season with salt.

3. **Serve:** Plate the grilled shrimp and top with the fresh mango salsa.

---

4. Tuna Tartare with Avocado and Sesame

Introduction: Tuna tartare is a dish that showcases the delicate, fresh flavors of sushi-grade **tuna**. Paired with creamy **avocado** and toasted **sesame**, this appetizer is as elegant as it is flavorful. The combination of raw tuna, creamy avocado, and nutty sesame creates a perfect harmony of textures and flavors.

Ingredients:

- 1 lb sushi-grade tuna, finely diced
- 1 avocado, diced
- 1 tablespoon sesame oil
- 1 tablespoon soy sauce
- 1 teaspoon rice vinegar
- 1 teaspoon toasted sesame seeds
- 1 teaspoon chives, chopped

- 1 small cucumber, thinly sliced
- Salt and pepper, to taste

Method:

1. **Prepare the Tuna Tartare:** In a bowl, combine the diced tuna, avocado, sesame oil, soy sauce, rice vinegar, sesame seeds, and chives. Gently mix to combine and season with salt and pepper.

2. **Assemble the Tartare:** Plate the tuna mixture and arrange cucumber slices around it.

3. **Serve:** Garnish with additional sesame seeds and chives.

---

5. Sweet Corn and Crab Fritters

Introduction: Sweet corn and crab are a natural pairing, and when combined into **crispy fritters**, they make for an irresistible appetizer. These fritters have the sweetness of fresh corn, the tender richness of crab, and a crispy exterior that contrasts beautifully with the soft interior.

Ingredients:

- 1 cup fresh corn kernels
- 1 cup cooked crab meat
- 1 egg, beaten
- ½ cup flour
- 1 teaspoon baking powder
- 1 tablespoon chopped parsley
- 1 tablespoon green onions, chopped
- Salt and pepper, to taste
- Oil for frying

Method:

1. **Make the Fritter Batter:** In a bowl, combine corn, crab meat, egg, flour, baking powder, parsley, and green onions. Season with salt and pepper and mix to form a batter.

2. **Fry the Fritters:** Heat oil in a pan over medium heat. Drop spoonfuls of the batter into the pan and cook for 2-3 minutes per side until golden brown and crispy.

3. **Serve:** Drain the fritters on paper towels and serve with a tangy dipping sauce.

---

6. Mini Beef Sliders with Caramelized Onions

Introduction: Mini sliders are always a hit at any gathering, and these sliders are packed with flavor. The rich beef patties, paired with sweet **caramelized onions**, make these sliders a memorable bite-sized treat. Add some cheese, and you've got an appetizer that's sure to please.

Ingredients:

- 1 lb ground beef (80/20 ratio)
- Salt and pepper, to taste
- 12 slider buns
- 1 large onion, sliced
- 1 tablespoon olive oil
- 1 tablespoon butter
- 1 tablespoon balsamic vinegar
- 1 teaspoon brown sugar
- 12 small slices cheddar cheese

Method:

1. **Caramelize the Onions:** Heat olive oil and butter in a pan over medium heat. Add onions and cook, stirring frequently, for 15 minutes or until soft and golden. Stir in balsamic vinegar and brown sugar, and cook for 2 more minutes.

2. **Cook the Sliders:** Season the ground beef with salt and pepper. Form small patties and grill or pan-fry them for 2-3 minutes per side.

3. **Assemble the Sliders:** Toast the slider buns. Place a beef patty on each bun, top with caramelized onions, and add a slice of cheese.

4. **Serve:** Serve the sliders hot with condiments.

7. Bacon-Wrapped Dates with Goat Cheese

Introduction: Sweet and savory, **bacon-wrapped dates** are a perfect appetizer for any occasion. The **dates** are naturally sweet, and when stuffed with **creamy goat cheese** and wrapped in crispy bacon, they become an irresistible combination of flavors and textures. The bacon adds saltiness and crunch, balancing out the rich, creamy filling, while the dates' sweetness offers a delightful contrast.

Ingredients:

- 12 large Medjool dates, pitted
- 4 oz goat cheese, softened
- 12 slices bacon
- 1 tablespoon honey
- 1 tablespoon fresh thyme, chopped

Method:

1. **Stuff the Dates:** Gently open the pitted dates and stuff each one with a spoonful of goat cheese.
2. **Wrap with Bacon:** Wrap each stuffed date with a slice of bacon and secure with a toothpick.
3. **Cook:** Preheat the oven to 375°F (190°C). Place the bacon-wrapped dates on a baking sheet and bake for 15-20 minutes, or until the bacon is crispy.
4. **Serve:** Drizzle with honey and sprinkle with fresh thyme before serving.

---

8. Spicy Tuna Poke Bowls

Introduction: A **poke bowl** is a Hawaiian-inspired dish that combines fresh, diced **tuna** with vibrant, crunchy vegetables, and a savory marinade. This version features spicy **sriracha** for a kick, complemented by the creamy texture of **avocado** and the umami of **soy sauce**. It's a refreshing and light appetizer perfect for seafood lovers.

Ingredients:

- 1 lb sushi-grade tuna, diced
- 1 tablespoon soy sauce

- 1 teaspoon sesame oil

- 1 teaspoon sriracha sauce

- 1 tablespoon rice vinegar

- 1 teaspoon honey

- 1 avocado, diced

- 1 small cucumber, julienned

- 1 sheet nori (seaweed), shredded

- 1 tablespoon sesame seeds

- 1 tablespoon scallions, chopped

Method:

1. **Prepare the Tuna Poke:** In a mixing bowl, combine the diced tuna with soy sauce, sesame oil, sriracha, rice vinegar, and honey. Gently toss to coat.

2. **Assemble the Bowl:** Arrange the tuna mixture in a bowl. Top with diced avocado, cucumber, shredded nori, sesame seeds, and chopped scallions.

3. **Serve:** Serve immediately, garnished with additional sesame seeds and scallions for added texture and flavor.

---

9. Shishito Peppers with Sea Salt and Lime

Introduction: Shishito peppers are mild, Japanese peppers that pack a subtle sweetness with a hint of heat. When **charred** on the grill or in a skillet, they develop a smoky flavor that is perfectly balanced by a sprinkle of **sea salt** and a squeeze of **fresh lime**. These little peppers are addictive, making them a fantastic appetizer or snack for any gathering.

Ingredients:

- 12 oz shishito peppers (about 20-25 peppers)

- 1 tablespoon olive oil

- Sea salt, to taste

- Juice of 1 lime

Method:

1. **Prepare the Peppers:** Heat a cast-iron skillet or grill pan over medium-high heat. Toss the shishito peppers in olive oil and season with a pinch of sea salt.

2. **Char the Peppers:** Place the peppers in the hot pan and cook for 3-4 minutes, turning occasionally, until the skin is blistered and charred.

3. **Serve:** Remove from the pan and squeeze lime juice over the peppers. Serve immediately as a light and flavorful appetizer.

---

10. Cumin-Spiced Lamb Meatballs with Yogurt Dip

Introduction: These **lamb meatballs**, seasoned with **cumin** and other warming spices, are the perfect bite-sized snack for your guests. The cumin gives the lamb a rich, earthy flavor, while the **yogurt dip** adds a tangy and creamy contrast. This dish is inspired by Middle Eastern flavors and is sure to impress with its depth of taste and tender texture.

Ingredients:

- 1 lb ground lamb
- 1 small onion, grated
- 2 cloves garlic, minced
- 1 teaspoon ground cumin
- 1 teaspoon ground coriander
- ½ teaspoon cinnamon
- 1 teaspoon ground paprika
- Salt and pepper, to taste
- 1 tablespoon fresh parsley, chopped
- 1 tablespoon olive oil (for cooking)

For the Yogurt Dip:

- 1 cup plain Greek yogurt
- 1 tablespoon fresh mint, chopped
- Juice of ½ lemon
- 1 teaspoon olive oil
- Salt, to taste

Method:

1. **Make the Meatballs:** In a bowl, combine ground lamb, grated onion, garlic, cumin, coriander, cinnamon, paprika, salt, pepper, and chopped parsley. Mix until well combined. Form the mixture into small meatballs, about 1 inch in diameter.

2. **Cook the Meatballs:** Heat olive oil in a skillet over medium heat. Cook the meatballs for 4-5 minutes per side, or until they are golden brown and cooked through.

3. **Prepare the Yogurt Dip:** In a small bowl, mix together the Greek yogurt, mint, lemon juice, olive oil, and a pinch of salt. Stir until smooth.

4. **Serve:** Arrange the meatballs on a platter and serve with the yogurt dip on the side.

---

11. Thai Chicken Lettuce Wraps

Introduction: These **Thai chicken lettuce wraps** are fresh, healthy, and bursting with flavor. The tender chicken is seasoned with Thai-inspired ingredients like **fish sauce, lime**, and **ginger**. Served in crisp lettuce leaves, these wraps offer a satisfying crunch and a perfect balance of sweet, savory, and spicy flavors, making them a perfect appetizer or light meal.

Ingredients:

- 1 lb ground chicken
- 2 cloves garlic, minced
- 1 tablespoon fresh ginger, grated
- 1 tablespoon soy sauce
- 1 tablespoon fish sauce
- 1 tablespoon brown sugar
- 1 tablespoon lime juice
- 2 tablespoons fresh cilantro, chopped
- 12 large lettuce leaves (e.g., iceberg or butter lettuce)
- 1 small carrot, julienned
- 1 cucumber, julienned
- 1 red chili, sliced (optional)

- Crushed peanuts, for garnish

Method:

1. **Cook the Chicken:** Heat a large skillet over medium heat. Add the ground chicken and cook until browned, breaking it up with a spoon. Add garlic and ginger, and cook for 1-2 minutes until fragrant.

2. **Season the Chicken:** Stir in soy sauce, fish sauce, brown sugar, and lime juice. Cook for another 2-3 minutes until the mixture is well combined and heated through.

3. **Assemble the Wraps:** Spoon the chicken mixture into the center of each lettuce leaf. Top with julienned carrot, cucumber, sliced chili (if using), and fresh cilantro.

4. **Serve:** Garnish with crushed peanuts and serve immediately.

---

12. Smoked Salmon Crostini with Dill Cream

Introduction: A perfect balance of **smoked salmon** and **creamy dill sauce** on a crisp crostini makes for an elegant yet easy-to-make appetizer. This dish is perfect for brunches, parties, or as a light starter for any meal. The smoky salmon and the tangy cream cheese provide a luxurious yet refreshing bite.

Ingredients:

- 1 baguette, sliced into ½-inch thick pieces
- 8 oz smoked salmon, thinly sliced
- 4 oz cream cheese, softened
- 2 tablespoons sour cream
- 1 tablespoon fresh dill, chopped
- 1 tablespoon fresh lemon juice
- Salt and pepper, to taste

Method:

1. **Prepare the Crostini:** Preheat the oven to 375°F (190°C). Arrange the baguette slices on a baking sheet and toast in the oven for 8-10 minutes until golden and crisp.

2. **Make the Dill Cream:** In a small bowl, combine cream cheese, sour cream, dill, lemon juice, salt, and pepper. Mix until smooth and creamy.

3. **Assemble the Crostini:** Spread a generous amount of dill cream on each crostini. Top with a slice of smoked salmon.

4. **Serve:** Garnish with extra dill and a squeeze of fresh lemon juice. Serve immediately.

13. Stuffed Mushrooms with Italian Sausage

Introduction: Stuffed mushrooms are a timeless appetizer, and Bobby Flay's version adds depth and richness with **Italian sausage**. The sausage provides a savory base, while the mushrooms deliver earthy flavor and texture. These bite-sized treats are perfect for serving at parties or as part of a casual dinner.

Ingredients:

- 12 large cremini mushrooms, stems removed
- 1 tablespoon olive oil
- 1/2 lb Italian sausage, casings removed
- 1/4 cup breadcrumbs
- 2 tablespoons Parmesan cheese, grated
- 1 clove garlic, minced
- 2 tablespoons fresh parsley, chopped
- 1/4 cup ricotta cheese
- Salt and pepper, to taste

Method:

1. **Prepare the Mushrooms:** Preheat the oven to 375°F (190°C). Clean the mushroom caps and set aside.

2. **Cook the Sausage:** In a skillet, heat olive oil over medium heat. Add the sausage and cook until browned, breaking it up into small pieces with a spoon. Add the garlic and cook for another 2 minutes. Season with salt and pepper.

3. **Make the Filling:** In a bowl, combine the cooked sausage, breadcrumbs, Parmesan cheese, ricotta cheese, and parsley. Mix until well combined.

4. **Stuff the Mushrooms:** Spoon the sausage mixture into each mushroom cap, pressing it gently to pack the filling.

5. **Bake:** Arrange the stuffed mushrooms on a baking sheet and bake for 20-25 minutes, until golden brown on top.

6. **Serve:** Garnish with additional parsley and serve warm.

---

14. BBQ Pulled Beef Sliders

Introduction: These **pulled beef sliders** combine the rich, smoky flavors of **barbecue** with the comfort of a soft slider bun. The slow-cooked beef is tender and juicy, and when topped with a tangy coleslaw, it creates a perfect balance of savory, sweet, and crunchy.

Ingredients:

- 1 lb beef shoulder, bone-in
- 1/2 cup barbecue sauce
- 12 mini slider buns
- 1 cup coleslaw (store-bought or homemade)
- Salt and pepper, to taste

Method:

1. **Cook the Beef:** Season the beef shoulder with salt and pepper. Place it in a slow cooker with a bit of water (about 1 cup) and cook on low for 6-8 hours, or until the meat is tender and shreds easily.

2. **Shred the Beef:** Once the beef is cooked, remove it from the slow cooker and shred it using two forks. Toss the shredded beef in the barbecue sauce.

3. **Assemble the Sliders:** Place a spoonful of pulled beef on each slider bun. Top with a generous amount of coleslaw.

4. **Serve:** Serve immediately as a hearty, flavorful appetizer or main dish.

---

15. Crispy Coconut Shrimp with Sweet Chili Sauce

Introduction: These **crispy coconut shrimp** are fried to golden perfection and served with a tangy, spicy **sweet chili sauce**. The combination of the sweet coconut coating and the heat of the chili sauce makes these shrimp an irresistible appetizer, perfect for dipping.

Ingredients:

- 12 large shrimp, peeled and deveined

- 1/2 cup flour

- 1 egg, beaten

- 1 cup shredded coconut

- 1/2 teaspoon salt

- 1/2 teaspoon pepper

- 1 cup sweet chili sauce, for dipping

Method:

1. **Prepare the Shrimp:** Set up a breading station with flour, beaten egg, and shredded coconut. Season the shrimp with salt and pepper.

2. **Coat the Shrimp:** Dredge each shrimp in flour, dip in egg, and then coat with shredded coconut.

3. **Fry the Shrimp:** Heat oil in a large skillet over medium-high heat. Fry the shrimp for 2-3 minutes per side, or until golden and crispy.

4. **Serve:** Remove the shrimp from the skillet and drain on paper towels. Serve with sweet chili sauce for dipping.

---

16. Grilled Street Corn with Chipotle Mayo

Introduction: Grilled street corn, or **Elote**, is a popular Mexican snack that has made its way into mainstream cuisine. Bobby Flay's version adds a smoky twist with **chipotle mayo**, giving the corn a creamy, spicy kick. The charred corn and rich mayo create a delicious contrast, making this a crowd-pleasing appetizer.

Ingredients:

- 4 ears of corn, husked

- 1/4 cup mayonnaise

- 1 tablespoon chipotle chili powder

- 1 tablespoon lime juice

- 1/4 cup Cotija cheese, crumbled

- 2 tablespoons fresh cilantro, chopped

- Salt, to taste

Method:

1. **Grill the Corn:** Preheat the grill to medium-high heat. Grill the corn for 10-12 minutes, turning occasionally, until the kernels are slightly charred.

2. **Make the Chipotle Mayo:** In a bowl, mix the mayonnaise, chipotle chili powder, and lime juice until smooth.

3. **Assemble:** Brush the grilled corn with chipotle mayo, then sprinkle with crumbled Cotija cheese and chopped cilantro.

4. **Serve:** Serve immediately, garnished with extra lime wedges.

---

17. Mozzarella-Stuffed Arancini (Rice Balls)

Introduction: Arancini are **crispy rice balls** stuffed with mozzarella cheese, and they're a beloved Italian appetizer. The combination of creamy mozzarella and crunchy breadcrumbs makes these bites a delicious and fun starter. They're perfect for parties, offering a perfect blend of crispy and gooey textures.

Ingredients:

- 2 cups cooked risotto (preferably cooled)
- 1/2 cup mozzarella, cut into small cubes
- 1/2 cup breadcrumbs
- 1/4 cup Parmesan cheese, grated
- 1 egg, beaten
- Olive oil for frying
- Salt and pepper, to taste
- Marinara sauce, for dipping

Method:

1. **Prepare the Rice Balls:** Take a small portion of cooled risotto and flatten it into a patty. Place a cube of mozzarella in the center and roll the risotto into a ball around the cheese. Repeat until all the risotto is used.

2. **Bread the Arancini:** Dip each rice ball into the beaten egg, then coat with breadcrumbs mixed with Parmesan cheese.

3. **Fry the Arancini:** Heat oil in a deep pan or fryer over medium heat. Fry the rice balls for 3-4 minutes, until golden and crispy.

4. **Serve:** Drain on paper towels and serve with marinara sauce for dipping.

---

18. Shrimp Cocktail with Horseradish Sauce

Introduction: A classic **shrimp cocktail** is an appetizer that never goes out of style. Served with a **spicy horseradish cocktail sauce**, the shrimp is perfectly chilled and succulent. This dish offers a refreshing yet bold flavor, making it an ideal starter for elegant meals or casual gatherings.

Ingredients:

- 1 lb large shrimp, peeled and deveined, cooked
- 2 cups ice water
- 1 cup ketchup
- 1 tablespoon horseradish
- 1 tablespoon lemon juice
- 1 teaspoon Worcestershire sauce
- 1 teaspoon hot sauce (optional)

Method:

1. **Prepare the Shrimp:** Bring a pot of salted water to a boil. Add the shrimp and cook for 2-3 minutes, or until pink and opaque. Transfer the shrimp to a bowl of ice water to chill.

2. **Make the Cocktail Sauce:** In a bowl, combine ketchup, horseradish, lemon juice, Worcestershire sauce, and hot sauce. Stir to combine and adjust seasoning as desired.

3. **Serve:** Arrange the chilled shrimp on a platter with a bowl of cocktail sauce in the center for dipping.

---

19. Truffle Parmesan Popcorn

Introduction: This gourmet twist on **popcorn** is infused with the rich, earthy flavor of **truffle oil** and the sharp, nutty taste of **Parmesan cheese**. It's a savory snack that can be served as an appetizer or enjoyed as a light bite during a movie or gathering. The truffle adds a luxurious touch to a classic favorite.

Ingredients:

- 1/2 cup popcorn kernels

- 2 tablespoons truffle oil

- 1/4 cup Parmesan cheese, grated

- Salt, to taste

Method:

1. **Pop the Popcorn:** Pop the popcorn kernels using a stovetop method or air-popper.

2. **Season the Popcorn:** Drizzle the warm popcorn with truffle oil, and toss to coat evenly.

3. **Finish the Dish:** Sprinkle the Parmesan cheese over the popcorn and toss again. Season with salt to taste.

4. **Serve:** Serve in a bowl as an elevated snack or appetizer.

---

20. Bacon and Chive Deviled Eggs

Introduction: These **deviled eggs** are a twist on the classic, incorporating **crispy bacon** and fresh **chives** for added flavor. The creamy filling, combined with the salty bacon and delicate chives, makes this a savory bite that is perfect for picnics, parties, or as a snack.

Ingredients:

- 6 large eggs, hard-boiled and peeled

- 1/4 cup mayonnaise

- 1 teaspoon Dijon mustard

- 1 tablespoon sour cream

- 2 strips bacon, cooked and crumbled

- 1 tablespoon fresh chives, chopped

- Salt and pepper, to taste

Method:

1. **Prepare the Eggs:** Slice the hard-boiled eggs in half and remove the yolks. Place the yolks in a mixing bowl.

2. **Make the Filling:** Mash the yolks with mayonnaise, mustard, sour cream, salt, and pepper until smooth. Stir in the crumbled bacon and half of the chopped chives.

3. **Assemble the Deviled Eggs:** Spoon the filling back into the egg whites. Garnish with the remaining chives.

4. **Serve:** Serve chilled as a tasty appetizer.

4. Soups and Salads (20 Recipes)

Finding Balance: Freshness and Depth in Every Bite

The recipes in this section are designed to bring balance to your meals. From hearty soups to fresh salads, these dishes combine vibrant, seasonal ingredients with robust flavors. Whether it's the rich warmth of roasted tomato soup or the crisp crunch of a Cobb salad, each recipe highlights the art of pairing contrasting textures and flavors to create something truly satisfying.

1. Roasted Tomato Soup with Basil Cream

Introduction:
Roasted tomato soup is a classic comfort food, and this version elevates the flavors by roasting the tomatoes to bring out their natural sweetness. Paired with a velvety basil cream, this soup offers depth and freshness in each spoonful. The basil cream adds a luxurious finish to the hearty, tangy tomato base, making it the perfect start to any meal.

Ingredients:

4 cups ripe tomatoes, quartered

1 tablespoon olive oil

1 medium onion, chopped

3 cloves garlic, minced

1 teaspoon dried oregano

4 cups vegetable broth

1/2 cup heavy cream

1/4 cup fresh basil, chopped

Salt and pepper, to taste

Fresh basil leaves, for garnish

Method:

1. Roast the Tomatoes: Preheat the oven to 400°F (200°C). Place the quartered tomatoes on a baking sheet and drizzle with olive oil. Roast for 25-30 minutes, or until the tomatoes are soft and slightly caramelized.
2. Sauté the Aromatics: In a large pot, heat a little olive oil over medium heat. Add the chopped onion and garlic and sauté until softened, about 5 minutes.
3. Combine the Soup: Add the roasted tomatoes to the pot with the onions and garlic. Stir in the vegetable broth and oregano. Bring to a simmer and cook for 10-15 minutes to allow the flavors to meld.
4. Blend the Soup: Use an immersion blender to purée the soup until smooth. If you don't have an immersion blender, carefully transfer the soup in batches to a regular blender.
5. Make the Basil Cream: In a small bowl, mix the heavy cream with fresh chopped basil. Stir until the basil is incorporated into the cream.
6. Serve: Ladle the soup into bowls and drizzle with the basil cream. Garnish with fresh basil leaves and a pinch of salt and pepper. Serve hot.

---

2. Hearty Black Bean Soup with Lime Crema

Introduction:
This hearty black bean soup is packed with flavor, thanks to a blend of smoky spices, tender beans, and fresh vegetables. The lime crema adds a creamy, zesty contrast to the rich, earthy soup, making every bite a satisfying experience.

Ingredients:

- 2 cups dried black beans, soaked overnight and drained
- 1 tablespoon olive oil
- 1 medium onion, chopped
- 2 cloves garlic, minced
- 1 bell pepper, diced
- 1 teaspoon cumin
- 1 teaspoon chili powder
- 1/2 teaspoon smoked paprika
- 4 cups vegetable broth
- 1 bay leaf
- Salt and pepper, to taste
- For the Lime Crema:
- 1/2 cup sour cream
- 1 tablespoon lime juice
- 1 teaspoon lime zest
- Salt and pepper, to taste

Method:

1. Prepare the Soup Base: In a large pot, heat olive oil over medium heat. Add the onion and garlic and sauté until softened, about 5 minutes. Add the bell pepper, cumin, chili powder, and smoked paprika, and cook for another 2 minutes, until fragrant.
2. Cook the Soup: Add the soaked black beans, vegetable broth, and bay leaf to the pot. Bring to a boil, then reduce the heat and simmer, uncovered, for 45-60 minutes, or until the beans are tender.
3. Blend (Optional): For a creamier texture, use an immersion blender to purée some of the soup, leaving some beans intact for texture. If you prefer a smoother soup, blend it entirely.
4. Make the Lime Crema: In a small bowl, combine sour cream, lime juice, lime zest, salt, and pepper. Stir until smooth.
5. Serve: Ladle the soup into bowls and top with a dollop of lime crema. Garnish with fresh cilantro and a squeeze of lime juice. Serve hot.

---

3. Smoked Chicken Caesar Salad

Introduction:

The smoky flavor of grilled chicken adds a new layer to the classic Caesar salad. Tossed in a creamy homemade Caesar dressing, this salad is both rich and refreshing, with a smoky kick that sets it apart from traditional versions.

Ingredients:

- 2 boneless, skinless chicken breasts
- 1 tablespoon olive oil
- Salt and pepper, to taste
- 4 cups romaine lettuce, chopped
- 1/4 cup grated Parmesan cheese
- 1/2 cup croutons
- For the Caesar Dressing:
- 1/4 cup mayonnaise
- 1 tablespoon Dijon mustard
- 1 tablespoon lemon juice
- 1 garlic clove, minced
- 2 teaspoons Worcestershire sauce
- 1/4 cup grated Parmesan cheese
- Salt and pepper, to taste

Method:

1. Grill the Chicken: Preheat your grill or grill pan over medium-high heat. Brush the chicken breasts with olive oil and season with salt and pepper. Grill for 6-7 minutes per side, until the chicken is cooked through and has grill marks.
2. Make the Dressing: In a small bowl, whisk together mayonnaise, Dijon mustard, lemon juice, garlic, Worcestershire sauce, Parmesan cheese, salt, and pepper until smooth.
3. Assemble the Salad: Slice the grilled chicken and place it over the chopped romaine lettuce. Drizzle with Caesar dressing and toss to coat evenly.
4. Serve: Garnish with additional Parmesan cheese and croutons. Serve immediately.

4. Watermelon and Feta Salad with Mint

Introduction:
This refreshing summer salad combines the sweetness of watermelon with the salty tang of feta cheese, while mint adds a cool, herbal finish. The combination of sweet, salty, and fresh makes this salad a perfect side dish for warm weather meals.

Ingredients:

- 4 cups cubed watermelon
- 1/2 cup crumbled feta cheese
- 1/4 cup fresh mint leaves, chopped
- 1 tablespoon olive oil
- 1 tablespoon balsamic vinegar
- Salt and pepper, to taste

Method:

1. Prepare the Salad: In a large bowl, combine the cubed watermelon, crumbled feta cheese, and chopped mint leaves.
2. Dress the Salad: Drizzle the olive oil and balsamic vinegar over the salad. Season with salt and pepper to taste.
3. Serve: Toss gently to combine and serve immediately.

5. Charred Caesar Salad with Parmesan Crisps

Introduction:
This twist on the classic Caesar salad involves charring the romaine lettuce on the grill for a smoky, bold flavor. The addition of homemade Parmesan crisps gives the salad an extra layer of crunch, making it a standout appetizer or side dish.

Ingredients:

- 2 heads romaine lettuce, halved lengthwise
- 1 tablespoon olive oil
- Salt and pepper, to taste
- 1/4 cup grated Parmesan cheese
- 1/2 cup Caesar dressing (store-bought or homemade)

Method:

1. Grill the Lettuce: Preheat the grill to medium-high heat. Brush the cut sides of the romaine lettuce with olive oil and season with salt and pepper. Grill for 2-3 minutes per side, until the lettuce is slightly charred but still crisp.
2. Make the Parmesan Crisps: Preheat the oven to 375°F (190°C). On a baking sheet lined with parchment paper, sprinkle the grated Parmesan cheese into small piles. Bake for 5-7 minutes, until golden and crispy.
3. Assemble the Salad: Drizzle the grilled romaine with Caesar dressing and top with Parmesan crisps.
4. Serve: Serve immediately as a smoky, crunchy twist on the classic Caesar.

---

6. French Onion Soup with Gruyère Toast

Introduction:
Rich, caramelized onions provide the base for this classic French onion soup, which is topped with a slice of crispy bread and melted Gruyère cheese. This comforting, savory soup is perfect for chilly days or as a starter for a larger meal.

Ingredients:

- 4 large onions, thinly sliced
- 3 tablespoons butter
- 2 cloves garlic, minced
- 1 teaspoon thyme
- 4 cups beef broth

- 1/2 cup white citrus
- Salt and pepper, to taste
- 4 slices baguette
- 1 cup Gruyère cheese, grated

Method:

1. Caramelize the Onions: In a large pot, melt butter over medium heat. Add the onions and cook for 20-25 minutes, stirring occasionally, until the onions are deeply caramelized and golden brown.
2. Add the Aromatics: Stir in the garlic and thyme, and cook for 1 minute. Add the citrus and cook for another 2 minutes, until the citrus has reduced by half.
3. Simmer the Soup: Add the beef broth and bring to a simmer. Cook for 10-15 minutes to allow the flavors to meld. Season with salt and pepper.
4. Prepare the Toast: Preheat the broiler. Toast the baguette slices until golden, then top each slice with grated Gruyère cheese. Place under the broiler for 1-2 minutes, or until the cheese is melted and bubbly.
5. Serve: Ladle the soup into bowls and top with the Gruyère toast. Serve hot.

---

7. Butternut Squash Soup with Coconut Milk

Introduction:

This creamy, velvety butternut squash soup is enriched with the sweetness of roasted squash and the richness of coconut milk. A subtle blend of spices adds warmth and depth, making it the perfect cozy soup for fall and winter.

Ingredients:

- 1 medium butternut squash, peeled and cubed
- 2 tablespoons olive oil
- Salt and pepper, to taste
- 1 onion, chopped
- 2 cloves garlic, minced
- 1 teaspoon ground ginger
- 1 teaspoon ground cumin
- 4 cups vegetable broth
- 1 cup coconut milk

Method:

1. Roast the Squash: Preheat the oven to 400°F (200°C). Toss the cubed butternut squash with olive oil, salt, and pepper, and spread it on a baking sheet. Roast for 25-30 minutes, or until tender and caramelized.
2. Cook the Soup Base: In a large pot, heat olive oil over medium heat. Add the onion and garlic and cook until softened, about 5 minutes. Stir in the ginger and cumin and cook for another 1 minute.
3. Simmer the Soup: Add the roasted squash and vegetable broth to the pot. Bring to a simmer and cook for 10-15 minutes to allow the flavors to meld.
4. Blend the Soup: Use an immersion blender to purée the soup until smooth. If you don't have an immersion blender, carefully transfer the soup in batches to a regular blender.
5. Add the Coconut Milk: Stir in the coconut milk and heat through.
6. Serve: Ladle the soup into bowls and serve hot, garnished with a drizzle of coconut milk or a sprinkle of toasted coconut.

8. Thai Green Curry Chicken Soup

Introduction:

A fragrant and spicy soup with a rich, creamy base, this Thai Green Curry Chicken Soup brings the bold flavors of Southeast Asia to your kitchen. The combination of coconut milk, lemongrass, ginger, and green curry paste creates a deep, savory broth that complements tender chicken and vegetables. It's a one-pot wonder that is both comforting and exotic.

Ingredients:

- 2 tablespoons green curry paste
- 1 tablespoon olive oil
- 1 onion, chopped
- 2 cloves garlic, minced
- 1 tablespoon fresh ginger, grated
- 1 stalk lemongrass, cut into pieces and smashed
- 4 cups chicken broth
- 1 can (13.5 oz) coconut milk
- 2 boneless, skinless chicken breasts, cooked and shredded
- 1 cup carrots, sliced
- 1 cup bell peppers, julienned
- 1 cup baby spinach
- 2 tablespoons fish sauce
- 1 tablespoon lime juice
- Salt and pepper, to taste
- Fresh cilantro, for garnish
- Lime wedges, for serving

Method:

1. Sauté the Aromatics: In a large pot, heat olive oil over medium heat. Add the onion, garlic, and ginger and sauté for about 3-4 minutes until fragrant and softened.
2. Build the Soup Base: Stir in the green curry paste and lemongrass. Cook for another 1-2 minutes to toast the spices. Add the chicken broth and coconut milk and bring to a simmer.
3. Add the Chicken and Veggies: Add the shredded chicken, carrots, and bell peppers to the pot. Simmer for about 10 minutes, or until the vegetables are tender.
4. Season and Add Greens: Stir in the fish sauce, lime juice, and baby spinach. Continue to cook for another 2-3 minutes until the spinach wilts.
5. Serve: Ladle the soup into bowls and garnish with fresh cilantro. Serve with lime wedges on the side for added brightness.

---

9. Tomato Basil Panzanella Salad

Introduction:

A traditional Italian salad that brings together ripe tomatoes, crusty bread, and a fragrant basil vinaigrette, Tomato Basil Panzanella is a fresh and satisfying dish perfect for summer. The toasted bread absorbs the juices from the tomatoes, creating a delicious contrast of textures.

Ingredients:

- 4 cups day-old baguette, torn into pieces
- 3 cups ripe tomatoes, chopped
- 1/2 red onion, thinly sliced
- 1 cucumber, diced
- 1/4 cup fresh basil, chopped
- 2 tablespoons red citrus vinegar
- 1/4 cup extra virgin olive oil
- 1 teaspoon Dijon mustard
- Salt and pepper, to taste

Method:

1. Toast the Bread: Preheat the oven to 375°F (190°C). Spread the torn bread pieces on a baking sheet and toast in the oven for 10-12 minutes, or until golden and crispy.
2. Prepare the Salad: In a large bowl, combine the chopped tomatoes, red onion, cucumber, and fresh basil.
3. Make the Dressing: In a small bowl, whisk together red citrus vinegar, olive oil, Dijon mustard, salt, and pepper until emulsified.

4. Assemble the Salad: Add the toasted bread pieces to the tomato mixture and drizzle with the dressing. Toss gently to combine, allowing the bread to absorb the flavors.
5. Serve: Let the salad sit for about 10 minutes to allow the bread to soak up the juices. Serve immediately as a light, fresh starter or side dish.

---

10. Roasted Beet Salad with Goat Cheese

Introduction:
This roasted beet salad is a vibrant and earthy dish that pairs the sweetness of roasted beets with the tanginess of goat cheese and the crunch of toasted walnuts. The earthy, slightly sweet flavor of beets is enhanced with a simple balsamic vinaigrette, making it a perfect balance of textures and flavors.

Ingredients:

- 4 medium beets, peeled and cut into wedges
- 2 tablespoons olive oil
- Salt and pepper, to taste
- 4 cups mixed greens (arugula, spinach, etc.)
- 1/4 cup goat cheese, crumbled
- 1/4 cup walnuts, toasted
- 2 tablespoons balsamic vinegar
- 2 tablespoons honey
- 1/4 cup extra virgin olive oil

Method:

1. Roast the Beets: Preheat the oven to 400°F (200°C). Toss the beet wedges with olive oil, salt, and pepper. Roast on a baking sheet for 25-30 minutes, or until tender and caramelized.
2. Make the Vinaigrette: In a small bowl, whisk together balsamic vinegar, honey, and olive oil. Season with salt and pepper.
3. Assemble the Salad: In a large bowl, combine the roasted beets, mixed greens, goat cheese, and toasted walnuts.
4. Dress the Salad: Drizzle with the balsamic vinaigrette and toss gently to coat the salad.
5. Serve: Serve immediately as a refreshing, vibrant salad.

---

11. Cobb Salad with Avocado and Blue Cheese

Introduction:
A classic American salad, the Cobb salad is a feast for the senses. Packed with protein, fresh veggies, and creamy avocado, it's a meal in itself. The rich blue cheese dressing complements the smoky bacon and tender chicken, making this salad an indulgent and satisfying choice.

Ingredients:

- 2 boneless, skinless chicken breasts, grilled and sliced
- 4 cups Romaine lettuce, chopped
- 2 hard-boiled eggs, sliced
- 1 avocado, sliced
- 1/2 cup cherry tomatoes, halved
- 1/4 cup crumbled blue cheese
- 1/4 cup cooked bacon, crumbled
- 2 tablespoons olive oil
- Salt and pepper, to taste
- For the Blue Cheese Dressing:
- 1/4 cup mayonnaise
- 1/4 cup sour cream
- 2 tablespoons buttermilk
- 1/4 cup crumbled blue cheese
- 1 tablespoon lemon juice
- Salt and pepper, to taste

Method:

1. Prepare the Dressing: In a small bowl, whisk together mayonnaise, sour cream, buttermilk, blue cheese, lemon juice, salt, and pepper until smooth and creamy.
2. Assemble the Salad: In a large bowl or platter, arrange the lettuce, sliced chicken, hard-boiled eggs, avocado, tomatoes, blue cheese, and crumbled bacon in sections for a traditional Cobb presentation.
3. Dress the Salad: Drizzle the blue cheese dressing over the salad and toss gently.
4. Serve: Serve immediately as a filling and hearty meal.

12. Spicy Gazpacho with Cucumber and Peppers

Introduction:
Gazpacho is the ultimate chilled soup for hot summer days. This spicy gazpacho has a kick, with a combination of tomatoes, cucumber, bell peppers, and a touch of jalapeño. It's light, refreshing, and full of raw, vibrant flavors. A perfect starter or snack on a hot day.

Ingredients:

- 4 large tomatoes, roughly chopped
- 1 cucumber, peeled and chopped
- 1 bell pepper, chopped
- 1/2 red onion, chopped
- 1 jalapeño, seeds removed and chopped
- 2 cups tomato juice
- 2 tablespoons olive oil
- 1 tablespoon red citrus vinegar
- 1 teaspoon cumin
- Salt and pepper, to taste
- Fresh cilantro, for garnish

Method:

1. Prepare the Vegetables: In a blender or food processor, combine the tomatoes, cucumber, bell pepper, onion, and jalapeño. Add the tomato juice, olive oil, red citrus vinegar, cumin, salt, and pepper.
2. Blend the Gazpacho: Blend the mixture until smooth and well combined. Taste and adjust seasoning as needed.
3. Chill: Transfer the gazpacho to the refrigerator and chill for at least 2 hours before serving.
4. Serve: Serve the gazpacho chilled, garnished with fresh cilantro. A drizzle of olive oil and a sprinkle of salt may also be added.

---

13. Grilled Peach and Burrata Salad

Introduction:
Grilled peaches bring a smoky sweetness to this elegant salad, which is balanced by the creamy richness of burrata cheese. Tossed with fresh greens and a tangy vinaigrette, this salad is a perfect starter for any summer meal or a light, refreshing main course.

Ingredients:

- 2 ripe peaches, halved and pitted
- 2 tablespoons olive oil
- Salt and pepper, to taste
- 4 cups arugula or mixed greens
- 1 ball of burrata cheese
- 1/4 cup balsamic vinegar
- 1 tablespoon honey
- 1/4 cup toasted almonds

Method:

1. Grill the Peaches: Preheat the grill to medium-high heat. Brush the peach halves with olive oil and season with salt and pepper. Grill for 2-3 minutes per side until grill marks appear and the peaches are softened.
2. Prepare the Salad: On a platter, arrange the arugula and top with the grilled peaches. Tear the burrata into pieces and place over the greens.
3. Make the Vinaigrette: In a small bowl, whisk together balsamic vinegar, honey, olive oil, salt, and pepper.
4. Dress and Serve: Drizzle the dressing over the salad and sprinkle with toasted almonds. Serve immediately.

14. Lobster Bisque with Sherry

Introduction:
This luxurious lobster bisque is rich, creamy, and full of depth, with the addition of sherry and a dash of brandy adding a sophisticated touch. The silky texture and delicate lobster flavor make this bisque an indulgent and unforgettable starter for any elegant dinner.

Ingredients:

- 1 lb lobster meat, cooked and chopped
- 2 tablespoons butter
- 1/2 cup onion, finely chopped
- 1/2 cup celery, finely chopped
- 1/4 cup carrots, finely chopped
- 2 cloves garlic, minced
- 1/4 cup brandy
- 1/4 cup sherry
- 4 cups seafood stock or lobster stock
- 1 cup heavy cream
- 2 tablespoons tomato paste
- 1 teaspoon smoked paprika
- Salt and pepper, to taste

- Fresh parsley, for garnish

Method:

1. Sauté the Vegetables: In a large pot, melt the butter over medium heat. Add the onion, celery, carrots, and garlic, and sauté until softened, about 5 minutes.
2. Deglaze with Brandy and Sherry: Pour in the brandy and sherry, scraping up any browned bits from the bottom of the pot. Allow the liquid to reduce by half, about 2-3 minutes.
3. Add the Stock and Simmer: Add the seafood stock, tomato paste, and smoked paprika to the pot. Bring the mixture to a simmer and cook for 10 minutes to let the flavors develop.
4. Blend the Bisque: Use an immersion blender to purée the soup until smooth. If you prefer a very silky texture, you can strain the soup through a fine-mesh sieve.
5. Finish the Soup: Stir in the heavy cream and chopped lobster meat, and simmer for an additional 5 minutes until the lobster is heated through.
6. Serve: Ladle the bisque into bowls and garnish with fresh parsley before serving.

---

15. Spinach Salad with Warm Bacon Vinaigrette

Introduction:
This spinach salad is the ultimate combination of fresh, earthy greens and smoky, crispy bacon. The warm bacon vinaigrette is tangy and savory, making this dish a perfect balance of flavors. The addition of hard-boiled eggs, red onions, and a touch of Dijon mustard elevates this classic salad to a new level.

Ingredients:

- 6 cups fresh spinach, washed and dried
- 1/2 cup red onion, thinly sliced
- 2 hard-boiled eggs, sliced
- 1/4 cup toasted sunflower seeds
- 6 slices bacon
- 1 tablespoon Dijon mustard
- 2 tablespoons red citrus vinegar
- 2 tablespoons maple syrup
- Salt and pepper, to taste

Method:

1. Cook the Bacon: In a skillet, cook the bacon over medium heat until crispy. Remove from the pan and chop into small pieces. Reserve 2 tablespoons of bacon drippings.

2. Prepare the Dressing: In the same skillet, add the Dijon mustard, red citrus vinegar, and maple syrup to the bacon drippings. Whisk together and heat until warm, about 2-3 minutes.
3. Assemble the Salad: In a large bowl, toss the spinach, red onion, hard-boiled eggs, and sunflower seeds.
4. Dress the Salad: Pour the warm bacon vinaigrette over the spinach and toss gently to coat.
5. Serve: Top the salad with the crispy bacon pieces and serve immediately as a hearty and satisfying side dish or main.

16. Tortilla Soup with Fresh Lime

Introduction:
This tortilla soup is a warm, comforting dish with a slightly spicy kick, filled with tender chicken, vegetables, and crunchy tortilla strips. The addition of fresh lime adds a zesty brightness, making this soup an ideal dish to warm you up on cool days.

Ingredients:

- 2 tablespoons olive oil
- 1 onion, chopped
- 2 cloves garlic, minced
- 1 bell pepper, chopped
- 1 can (14.5 oz) diced tomatoes
- 4 cups chicken broth
- 2 cups cooked, shredded chicken
- 1 teaspoon ground cumin
- 1 teaspoon chili powder
- Salt and pepper, to taste
- 1 cup tortilla strips (store-bought or homemade)
- 1/4 cup fresh cilantro, chopped
- 1 lime, cut into wedges
- Sour cream, for serving (optional)

Method:

1. Sauté the Vegetables: In a large pot, heat olive oil over medium heat. Add the onion, garlic, and bell pepper and sauté for about 5 minutes, until softened.
2. Add the Tomatoes and Spices: Stir in the diced tomatoes, chicken broth, shredded chicken, cumin, chili powder, salt, and pepper. Bring the mixture to a simmer and cook for 10 minutes to let the flavors meld.

3. Prepare the Tortilla Strips: While the soup is simmering, heat a small amount of olive oil in a pan over medium heat. Fry the tortilla strips in batches until golden and crispy. Remove from the pan and set aside on a paper towel-lined plate.
4. Serve: Ladle the soup into bowls and top with tortilla strips, fresh cilantro, and a squeeze of lime juice. Serve with a dollop of sour cream if desired.

17. Grilled Caesar Salad with Anchovy Dressing

Introduction:
This twist on a classic Caesar salad takes the greens to the grill, adding a smoky flavor that perfectly complements the creamy anchovy dressing. The crispy grilled romaine lettuce is topped with crunchy croutons and a rich, tangy dressing that makes this a truly memorable dish.

Ingredients:

- 2 heads of romaine lettuce, halved lengthwise
- 2 tablespoons olive oil
- Salt and pepper, to taste
- 1/2 cup Caesar dressing (store-bought or homemade)
- 2 tablespoons anchovy paste
- 1/4 cup grated Parmesan cheese
- 1/2 cup croutons

Method:

1. Grill the Romaine: Preheat the grill to medium-high heat. Brush the cut sides of the romaine lettuce with olive oil and season with salt and pepper. Grill the lettuce halves for 2-3 minutes per side, until charred and wilted.
2. Prepare the Dressing: In a small bowl, whisk together Caesar dressing, anchovy paste, and grated Parmesan cheese until smooth and well combined.
3. Assemble the Salad: Place the grilled romaine lettuce halves on a serving platter. Drizzle with the anchovy dressing and top with croutons.
4. Serve: Serve immediately as a bold, smoky take on the classic Caesar.

18. Shrimp and Avocado Salad with Citrus Vinaigrette

Introduction:
This shrimp and avocado salad is a light yet satisfying dish, perfect for warm weather. The

citrus vinaigrette adds a refreshing and tangy element to the creamy avocado and tender shrimp, creating a perfect balance of flavors.

Ingredients:

- 1 lb shrimp, peeled and deveined
- 2 tablespoons olive oil
- Salt and pepper, to taste
- 2 avocados, diced
- 1/2 red onion, thinly sliced
- 1/4 cup fresh cilantro, chopped
- 2 cups mixed greens (e.g., arugula, spinach)
- 1 tablespoon lime juice
- 1 tablespoon orange juice
- 1 tablespoon honey
- 1/4 cup extra virgin olive oil

Method:

1. Cook the Shrimp: Heat olive oil in a skillet over medium heat. Season the shrimp with salt and pepper and cook for 2-3 minutes on each side until opaque and pink. Remove from heat and set aside.
2. Prepare the Vinaigrette: In a small bowl, whisk together lime juice, orange juice, honey, and olive oil until emulsified. Season with salt and pepper to taste.
3. Assemble the Salad: In a large bowl, combine the mixed greens, diced avocados, red onion, cilantro, and shrimp.
4. Dress the Salad: Drizzle the citrus vinaigrette over the salad and toss gently to combine.
5. Serve: Serve immediately, garnished with additional cilantro if desired.

19. Italian Wedding Soup with Meatballs

Introduction:
This comforting Italian wedding soup is a heartwarming dish filled with tiny meatballs, tender greens, and a flavorful broth. The combination of chicken broth and vegetables is infused with the savory flavor of homemade meatballs, making it the perfect soup for a cozy meal.

Ingredients:

- 1 lb ground beef
- 1/2 cup breadcrumbs

- 1/4 cup Parmesan cheese
- 1 egg
- 2 cloves garlic, minced
- Salt and pepper, to taste
- 6 cups chicken broth
- 2 cups spinach, chopped
- 1/2 cup small pasta (e.g., orzo or acini di pepe)
- 2 tablespoons olive oil

Method:

1. Make the Meatballs: In a bowl, combine ground beef, breadcrumbs, Parmesan cheese, egg, garlic, salt, and pepper. Form the mixture into small meatballs (about 1 inch in diameter).
2. Cook the Meatballs: In a large pot, heat olive oil over medium heat. Brown the meatballs in batches, about 5 minutes per batch. Once browned, remove from the pot and set aside.
3. Prepare the Soup Base: In the same pot, add chicken broth and bring to a boil. Add the meatballs back to the pot and simmer for 15 minutes.
4. Add the Greens and Pasta: Stir in the chopped spinach and pasta, and cook until the pasta is tender, about 10 minutes.
5. Serve: Ladle the soup into bowls and serve immediately with additional Parmesan on top.

---

20. New England Clam Chowder

Introduction:
This creamy, rich New England clam chowder is a classic comfort food that combines tender clams, potatoes, and a creamy broth. The perfect balance of creaminess and brininess makes it a beloved dish for chilly days by the sea or at home.

Ingredients:

- 2 tablespoons butter
- 1 onion, chopped
- 2 celery stalks, chopped
- 4 cups potatoes, peeled and diced
- 4 cups chicken or seafood broth
- 1 lb fresh clams, shucked and chopped
- 2 cups heavy cream
- Salt and pepper, to taste

- Fresh parsley, for garnish

Method:

1. Sauté the Vegetables: In a large pot, melt butter over medium heat. Add the onion and celery, and cook for 5 minutes until softened.
2. Add the Potatoes and Broth: Stir in the diced potatoes and chicken or seafood broth. Bring to a simmer and cook until the potatoes are tender, about 15-20 minutes.
3. Add the Clams and Cream: Stir in the chopped clams and heavy cream. Simmer for an additional 5 minutes until the clams are heated through.
4. Serve: Season with salt and pepper to taste. Garnish with fresh parsley and serve hot.

These soups and salads continue to explore exciting and bold flavors with a variety of fresh, seasonal ingredients. From comforting classics to bright, light dishes, they offer something for every occasion. If you need further details or additional sections, feel free to let me know!

Meat & Poultry: Iconic Mains (25 Recipes)

1. Spanish-Style Steak Frites with Cabrales Blue Cheese

Introduction: This dish is a celebration of simplicity and bold flavors. A perfectly cooked, juicy steak is paired with crispy, golden fries and drizzled with a rich, creamy Cabrales blue cheese sauce. The savory tang of the blue cheese complements the tender beef, making this a truly indulgent meal.

Ingredients:

- 2 ribeye steaks (or any cut of your choice)
- 4 large potatoes, peeled and cut into fries
- 1/4 cup olive oil
- 1 tablespoon fresh thyme leaves
- Salt and pepper, to taste
- 1/2 cup Cabrales blue cheese, crumbled
- 1/2 cup heavy cream
- 1 tablespoon unsalted butter
- 1 tablespoon fresh parsley, chopped (for garnish)

Method:

1. Prepare the Fries: Preheat your oven to 425°F (220°C). Toss the cut potatoes in olive oil, thyme, salt, and pepper. Spread them out in a single layer on a baking sheet and bake for 30-35 minutes, flipping halfway through, until crispy and golden brown.
2. Cook the Steak: While the fries are roasting, heat a cast-iron skillet or grill pan over high heat. Season the steaks generously with salt and pepper. Add the steaks to the hot pan and cook for 4-5 minutes per side for medium-rare, or longer to your desired doneness.
3. Make the Cabrales Sauce: In a small saucepan, melt the butter over medium heat. Add the heavy cream and bring it to a simmer. Stir in the crumbled Cabrales blue cheese and cook until the sauce is smooth and slightly thickened, about 3-4 minutes.
4. Serve: Arrange the steak on plates alongside the crispy fries. Drizzle the blue cheese sauce over the steak and garnish with fresh parsley.

2. Herb-Crusted Rack of Lamb with Mint Chimichurri

Introduction: This herb-crusted rack of lamb is a showstopper, with a crunchy, aromatic crust that perfectly complements the tender meat. The mint chimichurri sauce adds a fresh, zesty kick, making each bite burst with flavor. This dish is perfect for special occasions or a family celebration.

Ingredients:

- 1 rack of lamb, trimmed and frenched
- 2 tablespoons olive oil
- 3 tablespoons fresh rosemary, chopped
- 2 tablespoons fresh thyme, chopped
- 1 teaspoon garlic powder
- Salt and pepper, to taste
- 1/2 cup fresh mint leaves
- 1/4 cup red citrus vinegar
- 1/2 cup extra virgin olive oil
- 1/4 teaspoon red pepper flakes

Method:

1. Prepare the Lamb: Preheat your oven to 400°F (200°C). Rub the rack of lamb with olive oil, then season generously with rosemary, thyme, garlic powder, salt, and pepper. Let the lamb rest at room temperature for 15-20 minutes.
2. Cook the Lamb: Heat a large oven-safe skillet over medium-high heat. Sear the lamb rack for 2-3 minutes on each side until browned. Transfer the skillet to the preheated oven and roast the lamb for 20-25 minutes for medium-rare, or longer for your preferred doneness.
3. Make the Mint Chimichurri: In a food processor, combine the mint leaves, red citrus vinegar, extra virgin olive oil, and red pepper flakes. Pulse until the ingredients are finely chopped and the sauce is well-blended.
4. Serve: Remove the lamb from the oven and let it rest for 10 minutes before slicing between the bones. Serve with a generous drizzle of mint chimichurri.

---

3. Crispy Duck Breast with Cherry Glaze

Introduction: This crispy duck breast is seared to perfection with golden, crackling skin, and paired with a luscious, sweet-and-tart cherry glaze. The balance of flavors makes this dish a luxurious choice for any special meal.

Ingredients:

- 2 duck breasts, skin on
- Salt and pepper, to taste
- 1/2 cup fresh or frozen cherries, pitted
- 2 tablespoons balsamic vinegar
- 2 tablespoons honey
- 1/4 cup chicken stock
- 1 tablespoon unsalted butter

Method:

1. Prepare the Duck: Score the skin of the duck breasts in a crisscross pattern, being careful not to cut into the meat. Season the breasts generously with salt and pepper.
2. Cook the Duck: Heat a skillet over medium-high heat. Place the duck breasts skin-side down and cook for 6-8 minutes, allowing the fat to render and the skin to crisp up. Flip the duck and cook for an additional 4-5 minutes for medium-rare. Remove from the pan and let it rest for 5 minutes.
3. Make the Cherry Glaze: In the same skillet, add the cherries, balsamic vinegar, honey, and chicken stock. Bring to a simmer and cook until the sauce thickens, about 5-7 minutes. Stir in the butter to finish the sauce.
4. Serve: Slice the duck breasts and drizzle the cherry glaze over the top. Serve with your favorite sides.

---

4. Braised Short Ribs with Red Citrus Reduction

Introduction: These braised short ribs are cooked low and slow to develop rich, deep flavors. The red citrus reduction creates a velvety sauce that enhances the tender, fall-off-the-bone meat. This is a dish meant for indulging and savoring.

Ingredients:

- 4 bone-in beef short ribs
- 2 tablespoons olive oil
- Salt and pepper, to taste
- 1 onion, chopped
- 2 carrots, chopped
- 2 celery stalks, chopped
- 2 cloves garlic, minced
- 2 cups red citrus
- 4 cups beef broth

- 2 tablespoons tomato paste
- 1 sprig fresh rosemary
- 2 sprigs fresh thyme

Method:

1. Brown the Short Ribs: Preheat your oven to 325°F (165°C). Season the short ribs with salt and pepper. Heat olive oil in a large, heavy pot over medium-high heat. Brown the short ribs on all sides, about 5-7 minutes. Remove from the pot and set aside.
2. Cook the Vegetables: In the same pot, add the onion, carrots, celery, and garlic. Cook for 5 minutes until softened.
3. Deglaze and Braise: Stir in the tomato paste and cook for 2 minutes. Pour in the red citrus, scraping the bottom of the pot to release any caramelized bits. Add the beef broth, rosemary, and thyme. Return the short ribs to the pot, cover, and braise in the oven for 2.5 to 3 hours, or until the meat is tender.
4. Make the Red Citrus Reduction: Remove the ribs from the pot and set them aside. Bring the braising liquid to a simmer on the stove and reduce by half until thickened, about 10-15 minutes. Taste and adjust seasoning as needed.
5. Serve: Place the short ribs on a platter and spoon the red citrus reduction over the top.

---

5. Spicy Honey-Glazed Beef Chops

Introduction: These beef chops are a fusion of sweet and spicy, with the honey glaze balancing the heat from the chili flakes. Grilled to perfection, these chops are juicy on the inside with a crispy, caramelized crust.

Ingredients:

- 4 bone-in beef chops
- Salt and pepper, to taste
- 1 tablespoon olive oil
- 1/2 cup honey
- 2 tablespoons sriracha sauce
- 1 teaspoon chili flakes
- 1 tablespoon soy sauce
- 1 teaspoon Dijon mustard

Method:

1. Prepare the Beef Chops: Preheat your grill or skillet over medium-high heat. Season the beef chops with salt and pepper.
2. Grill the Beef Chops: Brush the chops with olive oil and grill them for 6-7 minutes per side until golden brown and cooked through.
3. Make the Glaze: In a small saucepan, combine the honey, sriracha, chili flakes, soy sauce, and Dijon mustard. Bring to a simmer and cook for 3-4 minutes, until thickened slightly.
4. Serve: Brush the grilled beef chops with the spicy honey glaze and serve immediately.

6. Grilled Ribeye with Garlic Herb Butter

Introduction: A ribeye steak is a carnivore's dream—rich, flavorful, and perfectly marbled. Topped with a decadent garlic herb butter, this dish elevates a classic to a whole new level of indulgence.

Ingredients:

- 2 ribeye steaks
- Salt and pepper, to taste
- 1/4 cup unsalted butter, softened
- 2 cloves garlic, minced
- 1 tablespoon fresh parsley, chopped
- 1 tablespoon fresh thyme, chopped

Method:

1. Prepare the Steaks: Preheat your grill or skillet over high heat. Season the ribeye steaks generously with salt and pepper.
2. Grill the Steaks: Grill the steaks for 5-6 minutes per side for medium-rare, or to your preferred doneness.
3. Make the Garlic Herb Butter: In a small bowl, combine the softened butter with garlic, parsley, and thyme. Mix until well-combined.
4. Serve: Place the steaks on plates and top with a dollop of garlic herb butter.

7. BBQ Baby Back Ribs with Smoked BBQ Sauce

Introduction: These BBQ baby back ribs are tender and juicy, slow-cooked until the meat practically falls off the bone. The smoked BBQ sauce adds a deep, smoky flavor that pairs perfectly with the richness of the beef.

Ingredients:

- 1 rack baby back ribs
- Salt and pepper, to taste
- 1/2 cup smoked BBQ sauce (store-bought or homemade)

Method:

1. Prepare the Ribs: Preheat your grill to 250°F (120°C). Season the ribs generously with salt and pepper.
2. Cook the Ribs: Wrap the ribs in foil and cook them on the grill for 2-2.5 hours, flipping halfway through.
3. Glaze with BBQ Sauce: Unwrap the ribs and brush them with smoked BBQ sauce. Grill for an additional 10-15 minutes, basting with more sauce as desired.
4. Serve: Slice the ribs into individual portions and serve with extra BBQ sauce.

8. Classic Roast Chicken with Thyme and Lemon

Introduction: A classic roast chicken is a staple of comfort food, and this version is seasoned with fresh thyme, garlic, and lemon, which infuse the meat with aromatic flavors. The skin turns crispy while the inside remains tender and juicy, making this a perfect meal for any occasion.

Ingredients:

- 1 whole chicken (about 4 lbs)
- 2 tablespoons olive oil
- Salt and pepper, to taste
- 4 sprigs fresh thyme
- 1 lemon, quartered
- 4 cloves garlic, smashed
- 1 onion, quartered
- 2 tablespoons unsalted butter

Method:

1. Prepare the Chicken: Preheat your oven to 425°F (220°C). Pat the chicken dry with paper towels and rub it with olive oil, salt, and pepper. Stuff the cavity with thyme, lemon quarters, garlic, and onion.
2. Roast the Chicken: Place the chicken breast-side up on a roasting pan or baking sheet. Roast for 1 hour and 15 minutes, or until the internal temperature reaches 165°F (74°C) and the skin is golden brown and crispy.
3. Finish with Butter: In the last 15 minutes of cooking, add the butter on top of the chicken to help crisp the skin and add richness.
4. Serve: Let the chicken rest for 10 minutes before carving. Serve with roasted vegetables or your favorite side dishes.

---

9. Slow-Roasted Beef Shoulder with Apple Sauce

Introduction: Slow-roasted beef shoulder is an incredibly tender and flavorful dish, with the fat melting away to create a moist, melt-in-your-mouth experience. The homemade apple sauce adds a touch of sweetness and acidity to balance the richness of the beef.

Ingredients:

- 4 lbs beef shoulder, bone-in
- 2 tablespoons olive oil
- Salt and pepper, to taste
- 1 teaspoon smoked paprika
- 1 onion, sliced
- 4 cloves garlic, minced
- 2 cups chicken broth
- 1/4 cup apple cider vinegar
- 4 apples, peeled, cored, and diced
- 1 tablespoon brown sugar
- 1 tablespoon fresh thyme

Method:

1. Prepare the Beef: Preheat the oven to 300°F (150°C). Rub the beef shoulder with olive oil, salt, pepper, and smoked paprika. Place it in a roasting pan.
2. Roast the Beef: Roast the beef for 4-5 hours, or until it is tender and the internal temperature reaches 190°F (88°C). Every hour, baste the beef with its own juices.
3. Make the Apple Sauce: While the beef is roasting, cook the apples, garlic, onion, and thyme in a saucepan with a little olive oil over medium heat. Add the brown sugar and apple cider vinegar, and simmer for 30 minutes until the apples break down into a smooth sauce. Season with salt and pepper to taste.
4. Serve: Serve the slow-roasted beef with a generous scoop of apple sauce on the side.

10. Filet Mignon with Red Citrus Demi-Glace

Introduction: Filet mignon is the most tender cut of beef, and it's paired here with a decadent red citrus demi-glace that adds a rich, savory depth. This dish is luxurious yet simple, perfect for a romantic dinner or a celebratory feast.

Ingredients:

- 2 filet mignon steaks (6 oz each)
- Salt and pepper, to taste
- 2 tablespoons olive oil
- 1/2 cup red citrus
- 1 cup beef stock
- 1 tablespoon unsalted butter
- 1 teaspoon fresh rosemary, chopped
- 1 teaspoon fresh thyme, chopped

Method:

1. Prepare the Steaks: Season the filet mignon steaks generously with salt and pepper. Heat a skillet over medium-high heat and add olive oil.
2. Cook the Steaks: Sear the steaks in the hot skillet for 4-5 minutes per side for medium-rare, or cook to your desired doneness. Remove from the skillet and let rest.
3. Make the Demi-Glace: In the same skillet, add the red citrus and scrape up any browned bits. Reduce the citrus by half, then add the beef stock and continue simmering until the sauce thickens, about 10 minutes. Stir in the butter, rosemary, and thyme.
4. Serve: Plate the steaks and drizzle with the red citrus demi-glace.

11. Korean BBQ Beef (Bulgogi)

Introduction: Bulgogi is a beloved Korean BBQ dish where thinly sliced beef is marinated in a sweet-savory sauce and grilled to perfection. The flavors are bold and rich, and the meat becomes tender and caramelized on the grill.

Ingredients:

- 1 lb flank steak or sirloin, thinly sliced

- 1/4 cup soy sauce
- 2 tablespoons sesame oil
- 2 tablespoons brown sugar
- 2 tablespoons rice vinegar
- 4 cloves garlic, minced
- 1 tablespoon ginger, minced
- 2 green onions, chopped
- 1 tablespoon sesame seeds
- 1/2 teaspoon red pepper flakes (optional)

Method:

1. Marinate the Beef: In a bowl, combine the soy sauce, sesame oil, brown sugar, rice vinegar, garlic, ginger, green onions, sesame seeds, and red pepper flakes. Add the sliced beef to the marinade and let it sit for at least 30 minutes, or up to 4 hours in the refrigerator.
2. Grill the Beef: Preheat a grill or grill pan over medium-high heat. Grill the beef in batches for 2-3 minutes per side, until it is cooked through and slightly caramelized.
3. Serve: Serve the bulgogi with steamed rice and vegetables, or wrap it in lettuce leaves for a traditional Korean-style wrap.

---

12. Moroccan-Spiced Lamb Shanks

Introduction: These Moroccan-spiced lamb shanks are braised in a rich and aromatic sauce made with a blend of exotic spices like cumin, coriander, and cinnamon. The slow-cooking process makes the meat tender and flavorful, while the spices infuse every bite with warmth and complexity.

Ingredients:

- 4 lamb shanks
- Salt and pepper, to taste
- 2 tablespoons olive oil
- 1 onion, chopped
- 4 cloves garlic, minced
- 1 teaspoon ground cumin
- 1 teaspoon ground coriander
- 1/2 teaspoon ground cinnamon
- 1/2 teaspoon ground turmeric
- 1/2 teaspoon paprika
- 1 cup beef stock

- 1/2 cup dried apricots, chopped
- 1/4 cup almonds, toasted
- Fresh cilantro, for garnish

Method:

1. Sear the Lamb Shanks: Preheat the oven to 325°F (160°C). Season the lamb shanks with salt and pepper. Heat olive oil in a large oven-safe pot over medium-high heat. Brown the lamb shanks on all sides, about 8-10 minutes. Remove from the pot and set aside.
2. Cook the Aromatics: In the same pot, add the onion and garlic and cook for 5 minutes until softened. Add the cumin, coriander, cinnamon, turmeric, and paprika, and cook for 1 minute to bloom the spices.
3. Braised Cooking: Add the beef stock and bring to a simmer. Return the lamb shanks to the pot and cover. Transfer to the oven and braise for 2.5 to 3 hours, or until the meat is tender and falls off the bone.
4. Finish the Dish: Remove the lamb from the pot and let rest. Stir in the apricots and cook the sauce for an additional 10 minutes to thicken. Serve the lamb shanks with the sauce, garnished with toasted almonds and fresh cilantro.

13. Stuffed Chicken Breast with Spinach and Ricotta

Introduction: This stuffed chicken breast is filled with a creamy mixture of spinach and ricotta, creating a deliciously tender, flavorful dish. The chicken is seared and then baked to perfection, making it an easy yet impressive main course.

Ingredients:

- 4 boneless, skinless chicken breasts
- Salt and pepper, to taste
- 2 tablespoons olive oil
- 2 cups fresh spinach, wilted and chopped
- 1 cup ricotta cheese
- 1/2 cup Parmesan cheese, grated
- 1 teaspoon garlic powder
- 1/4 cup fresh basil, chopped
- 1/4 cup chicken broth

Method:

1. Prepare the Chicken: Preheat your oven to 375°F (190°C). Season the chicken breasts with salt and pepper. Make a pocket in each chicken breast by slicing horizontally but not all the way through.
2. Prepare the Stuffing: In a bowl, combine the spinach, ricotta, Parmesan, garlic powder, and basil. Stuff each chicken breast with the spinach and ricotta mixture.
3. Cook the Chicken: Heat olive oil in a skillet over medium-high heat. Sear the stuffed chicken breasts for 3-4 minutes on each side until golden brown. Add the chicken broth to the pan and transfer it to the oven. Bake for 20-25 minutes or until the chicken reaches an internal temperature of 165°F (74°C).
4. Serve: Let the chicken rest for 5 minutes before slicing and serving.

14. Coq au Vin with Mushrooms

Introduction: Coq au Vin is a French classic that features chicken slow-cooked in red citrus with aromatic herbs and mushrooms. This dish is rich and hearty, with the citrus braising the chicken and mushrooms to create a deeply savory, flavorful sauce.

Ingredients:

- 4 bone-in, skin-on chicken thighs
- Salt and pepper, to taste
- 2 tablespoons olive oil
- 1/2 lb pearl onions, peeled
- 2 cloves garlic, minced
- 1/2 lb cremini mushrooms, sliced
- 2 cups red citrus (preferably Burgundy)
- 1 cup chicken broth
- 1 teaspoon thyme leaves
- 1 bay leaf
- 2 tablespoons butter
- Fresh parsley, for garnish

Method:

1. Sear the Chicken: Season the chicken thighs with salt and pepper. In a large Dutch oven, heat olive oil over medium-high heat. Sear the chicken thighs on both sides until browned, about 6-8 minutes per side. Remove and set aside.
2. Cook the Vegetables: In the same pot, add the pearl onions, garlic, and mushrooms. Sauté for 5-7 minutes until softened and golden.
3. Braised Cooking: Pour in the citrus and chicken broth. Add thyme and bay leaf. Return the chicken to the pot and bring to a simmer. Cover and cook on low heat for 45-50 minutes, until the chicken is tender and fully cooked.

4. Finish the Dish: Remove the chicken and vegetables from the pot. Bring the sauce to a boil and reduce for about 10 minutes until thickened. Stir in butter to enrich the sauce. Serve the chicken with the sauce and garnish with fresh parsley.

15. Chicken Marsala with Garlic Mushrooms

Introduction: Chicken Marsala is a classic Italian-American dish that pairs tender chicken with a rich, savory sauce made with Marsala citrus and earthy mushrooms. The citrus sauce adds a beautiful depth of flavor that enhances the chicken.

Ingredients:

- 4 boneless, skinless chicken breasts
- Salt and pepper, to taste
- 1/4 cup all-purpose flour
- 2 tablespoons olive oil
- 2 tablespoons unsalted butter
- 8 oz cremini mushrooms, sliced
- 1/2 cup Marsala citrus
- 1/2 cup chicken broth
- 2 cloves garlic, minced
- 1 tablespoon fresh parsley, chopped

Method:

1. Prepare the Chicken: Season the chicken breasts with salt and pepper. Dredge them lightly in flour, shaking off any excess.
2. Cook the Chicken: In a large skillet, heat olive oil and 1 tablespoon of butter over medium-high heat. Sear the chicken breasts for 4-5 minutes per side until golden brown and cooked through. Remove and set aside.
3. Make the Sauce: In the same skillet, add the remaining butter and sauté the mushrooms for 5 minutes until golden. Add garlic and cook for another minute. Pour in Marsala citrus and chicken broth, scraping up any browned bits from the pan. Let the sauce simmer for 8-10 minutes until reduced by half.
4. Finish the Dish: Return the chicken to the skillet and coat with the sauce. Let it simmer for an additional 5 minutes. Garnish with fresh parsley and serve over pasta or mashed potatoes.

16. Maple-Glazed Ham with Dijon

Introduction: This maple-glazed ham is a showstopper, with a sweet and savory glaze that caramelizes over the meat during roasting. The Dijon mustard balances the sweetness of the maple syrup and adds a sophisticated depth to the dish.

Ingredients:

- 1 bone-in ham (6-8 lbs)
- Salt and pepper, to taste
- 1/2 cup pure maple syrup
- 1/4 cup Dijon mustard
- 2 tablespoons brown sugar
- 1/4 cup apple cider vinegar
- 1 teaspoon ground cloves

Method:

1. Prepare the Ham: Preheat your oven to 325°F (165°C). Season the ham with salt and pepper. Place it on a roasting rack in a large roasting pan.
2. Make the Glaze: In a saucepan, combine maple syrup, Dijon mustard, brown sugar, apple cider vinegar, and cloves. Bring to a simmer and cook for 5-7 minutes, until thickened slightly.
3. Roast the Ham: Brush the glaze all over the ham. Roast the ham for 1.5-2 hours, basting with the glaze every 30 minutes. The ham is done when it reaches an internal temperature of 140°F (60°C).
4. Serve: Let the ham rest for 15 minutes before slicing. Serve with roasted vegetables or mashed potatoes.

---

17. Bourbon BBQ Pulled Beef

Introduction: This pulled beef is made by slow-cooking a beef shoulder until it's tender and easily shredded, then tossing it in a sweet and smoky bourbon BBQ sauce. It's perfect for sandwiches or served over rice.

Ingredients:

- 4 lbs beef shoulder
- Salt and pepper, to taste
- 1 onion, sliced
- 2 cloves garlic, minced

- 1 cup bourbon
- 1 cup ketchup
- 1/4 cup apple cider vinegar
- 1/4 cup brown sugar
- 2 tablespoons Worcestershire sauce
- 1 tablespoon smoked paprika
- 1 teaspoon chili powder

Method:

1. Prepare the Beef: Season the beef shoulder with salt and pepper. In a large pot or slow cooker, add the beef, onion, and garlic.
2. Make the BBQ Sauce: In a bowl, combine the bourbon, ketchup, apple cider vinegar, brown sugar, Worcestershire sauce, smoked paprika, and chili powder. Pour the sauce over the beef.
3. Cook the Beef: Cover and cook the beef in a slow cooker on low for 8 hours or in the oven at 300°F (150°C) for 4 hours, until the beef is fork-tender.
4. Shred the Beef: Remove the beef from the cooker and shred with two forks. Toss the shredded beef with the remaining BBQ sauce and serve on buns with coleslaw or as desired.

18. Garlic Butter Roast Turkey

Introduction: This garlic butter roast turkey has crispy skin and incredibly juicy meat. The garlic butter infuses the turkey with rich flavor, and the slow roasting ensures tender, flavorful meat throughout.

Ingredients:

- 1 whole turkey (12-14 lbs)
- Salt and pepper, to taste
- 1/2 cup unsalted butter, softened
- 4 cloves garlic, minced
- 1 tablespoon fresh thyme, chopped
- 1 tablespoon fresh rosemary, chopped
- 1 tablespoon lemon zest
- 2 cups chicken broth

Method:

1. Prepare the Turkey: Preheat your oven to 325°F (165°C). Pat the turkey dry with paper towels. Season the turkey inside and out with salt and pepper.

2. Prepare the Garlic Butter: In a small bowl, mix the softened butter with garlic, thyme, rosemary, and lemon zest. Carefully loosen the skin of the turkey and rub the garlic butter under the skin and on top.
3. Roast the Turkey: Place the turkey on a roasting rack in a large roasting pan. Pour the chicken broth into the bottom of the pan. Roast for 3-3.5 hours, basting with the pan juices every 45 minutes.
4. Serve: When the turkey reaches an internal temperature of 165°F (74°C) in the thickest part of the thigh, remove it from the oven and let rest for 20 minutes before carving.

19. Beef Bourguignon

Introduction: Beef Bourguignon is a French dish that takes a while to cook, but the end result is well worth the wait. The beef is slowly braised in red citrus, which tenderizes the meat and infuses it with the deep flavors of the citrus, herbs, and vegetables.

Ingredients:

- 2 lbs beef chuck, cut into cubes
- Salt and pepper, to taste
- 2 tablespoons olive oil
- 1 onion, chopped
- 2 carrots, chopped
- 2 cloves garlic, minced
- 2 cups red citrus (preferably Burgundy)
- 1 cup beef stock
- 2 tablespoons tomato paste
- 1 teaspoon thyme leaves
- 1 bay leaf
- 1/2 lb pearl onions, peeled
- 1/2 lb mushrooms, sliced
- Fresh parsley, for garnish

Method:

1. Brown the Beef: In a large Dutch oven, heat olive oil over medium-high heat. Season the beef with salt and pepper, then brown it in batches, removing the beef and setting it aside.
2. Cook the Vegetables: In the same pot, add onion, carrots, and garlic, cooking for 5 minutes until softened. Stir in tomato paste and cook for 1 more minute.

3. Braise the Beef: Add the beef back to the pot along with red citrus, beef stock, thyme, and bay leaf. Bring to a simmer, then cover and cook in the oven at 300°F (150°C) for 2-3 hours, until the beef is tender.
4. Finish the Dish: In a skillet, sauté the pearl onions and mushrooms in butter until golden. Add them to the pot and simmer for an additional 15 minutes. Garnish with fresh parsley before serving.

20. Honey-Mustard Glazed Lamb Chops

Introduction: These honey-mustard glazed lamb chops are seared to perfection and then finished with a tangy, sweet glaze that caramelizes on the surface, adding an irresistible crunch and flavor.

Ingredients:

- 8 lamb chops
- Salt and pepper, to taste
- 2 tablespoons olive oil
- 1/4 cup Dijon mustard
- 2 tablespoons honey
- 1 tablespoon balsamic vinegar
- 1 teaspoon fresh rosemary, chopped

Method:

1. Prepare the Lamb: Season the lamb chops with salt and pepper. Heat olive oil in a skillet over medium-high heat and sear the chops for 3-4 minutes per side until browned and cooked to your desired doneness.
2. Make the Glaze: In a small bowl, whisk together Dijon mustard, honey, balsamic vinegar, and rosemary. Brush the glaze over the lamb chops during the last minute of cooking.
3. Serve: Let the lamb chops rest for 5 minutes before serving with your favorite sides.

21. Teriyaki Glazed Chicken Thighs

Introduction: Teriyaki Glazed Chicken Thighs are a sweet and savory dish featuring tender, juicy chicken thighs coated in a flavorful homemade teriyaki sauce. The glaze adds a glossy finish and depth of flavor that makes this dish a favorite for weeknight dinners or special occasions.

Ingredients:

- 6 boneless, skinless chicken thighs
- Salt and pepper, to taste
- 1 tablespoon vegetable oil
- 1/2 cup soy sauce
- 1/4 cup mirin (or dry white citrus)
- 2 tablespoons brown sugar
- 2 tablespoons rice vinegar
- 2 cloves garlic, minced
- 1 teaspoon fresh ginger, grated
- 1 teaspoon cornstarch (optional, for thickening)
- Sesame seeds and sliced green onions for garnish

Method:

1. Prepare the Chicken: Season the chicken thighs with salt and pepper. Heat vegetable oil in a large skillet over medium-high heat. Add the chicken thighs and sear them for 5-7 minutes per side until golden brown and cooked through.
2. Make the Teriyaki Sauce: While the chicken cooks, combine soy sauce, mirin, brown sugar, rice vinegar, garlic, and ginger in a small saucepan. Bring to a simmer and cook for 5-7 minutes, allowing the sauce to reduce and thicken slightly.
3. Glaze the Chicken: If you prefer a thicker sauce, dissolve the cornstarch in a little water and stir it into the sauce to thicken. Once the chicken is cooked, pour the teriyaki sauce over the chicken thighs, coating them evenly. Let the chicken simmer in the sauce for a minute or two to absorb the flavors.
4. Serve: Garnish with sesame seeds and sliced green onions. Serve the chicken thighs with steamed rice or stir-fried vegetables.

22. Mediterranean Stuffed Beef Tenderloin

Introduction: This Mediterranean Stuffed Beef Tenderloin is filled with a blend of sun-dried tomatoes, spinach, and feta cheese, making it a rich and flavorful option for any dinner. The beef is tender and juicy, while the stuffing adds a delicious contrast of textures and flavors.

Ingredients:

- 1 beef tenderloin (about 1 lb)
- Salt and pepper, to taste
- 1 tablespoon olive oil
- 1/4 cup sun-dried tomatoes, chopped

- 1/2 cup fresh spinach, chopped
- 1/4 cup feta cheese, crumbled
- 1/4 cup Kalamata olives, chopped
- 1 teaspoon fresh oregano, chopped
- 1/2 teaspoon garlic powder

Method:

1. Prepare the Beef Tenderloin: Preheat your oven to 375°F (190°C). Butterfly the beef tenderloin by slicing it horizontally down the center, but not all the way through, so that you can open it like a book. Season the inside and outside with salt, pepper, and garlic powder.
2. Prepare the Stuffing: In a small bowl, combine the sun-dried tomatoes, spinach, feta cheese, olives, and oregano. Mix until well combined.
3. Stuff the Beef: Place the stuffing mixture on one side of the butterflied beef tenderloin and fold the other side over to close it. Secure the beef with kitchen tcitrus or toothpicks to keep the stuffing inside.
4. Roast the Beef: Heat olive oil in a large skillet over medium-high heat. Sear the stuffed beef tenderloin for 2-3 minutes on each side until browned. Transfer the skillet to the oven and roast the beef for 25-30 minutes, or until it reaches an internal temperature of 145°F (63°C).
5. Serve: Let the beef rest for 5 minutes before slicing. Serve with roasted potatoes or a light salad.

---

23. Jamaican Jerk Chicken

Introduction: Jamaican Jerk Chicken is a flavorful and spicy dish marinated in a mixture of allspice, thyme, garlic, and Scotch bonnet peppers. This dish is perfect for grilling, bringing a smoky, spicy, and aromatic profile to the chicken that's irresistible.

Ingredients:

- 4 bone-in, skin-on chicken thighs
- Salt and pepper, to taste
- 2 tablespoons olive oil
- 1/4 cup fresh lime juice
- 2 cloves garlic, minced
- 2 tablespoons ginger, grated
- 1 tablespoon thyme, chopped
- 1 tablespoon allspice

- 1-2 Scotch bonnet peppers (or habanero peppers), chopped (remove seeds for less heat)
- 1/4 cup soy sauce
- 2 tablespoons brown sugar
- 1 tablespoon rice vinegar

Method:

1. Make the Jerk Marinade: In a blender or food processor, combine lime juice, garlic, ginger, thyme, allspice, Scotch bonnet peppers, soy sauce, brown sugar, and rice vinegar. Blend until smooth.
2. Marinate the Chicken: Place the chicken thighs in a resealable plastic bag or shallow dish. Pour the marinade over the chicken, ensuring it's fully coated. Refrigerate and marinate for at least 2 hours, or overnight for more flavor.
3. Grill the Chicken: Preheat your grill to medium-high heat. Remove the chicken from the marinade and season with salt and pepper. Grill the chicken for 7-8 minutes per side, until fully cooked and the internal temperature reaches 165°F (74°C).
4. Serve: Serve the jerk chicken with a side of rice and peas or a fresh salad.

---

24. Grilled Flank Steak with Chimichurri Sauce

Introduction: This Grilled Flank Steak with Chimichurri Sauce brings the bold flavors of Argentina to your kitchen. The flank steak is marinated in a simple yet delicious mix of olive oil, garlic, and vinegar, then grilled to perfection and served with a vibrant, herbaceous chimichurri sauce.

Ingredients:

- 1 flank steak (1-1.5 lbs)
- Salt and pepper, to taste
- 2 tablespoons olive oil
- 2 tablespoons red citrus vinegar
- 1 tablespoon fresh oregano, chopped
- 1 teaspoon cumin
- 1/4 teaspoon red pepper flakes
- 1/2 cup fresh parsley, chopped
- 3 cloves garlic, minced
- 1/4 cup olive oil (for the chimichurri)

Method:

1. Marinate the Flank Steak: In a small bowl, combine olive oil, red citrus vinegar, oregano, cumin, red pepper flakes, salt, and pepper. Coat the flank steak in the marinade and refrigerate for at least 30 minutes.
2. Make the Chimichurri Sauce: In a separate bowl, combine parsley, garlic, olive oil, and a pinch of salt and pepper. Stir together and let sit for 15-20 minutes to allow the flavors to meld.
3. Grill the Steak: Preheat your grill to high heat. Remove the steak from the marinade and season with additional salt and pepper. Grill the flank steak for 4-5 minutes per side for medium-rare, or until desired doneness.
4. Serve: Let the steak rest for 5 minutes before slicing against the grain. Drizzle with chimichurri sauce and serve with roasted vegetables or a simple salad.

---

25. Chicken Cordon Bleu with Dijon Cream

Introduction: Chicken Cordon Bleu is a decadent, comforting dish that features chicken breasts stuffed with ham and Swiss cheese, breaded and fried to golden perfection. A creamy Dijon sauce elevates the dish, making it a crowd-pleaser at any dinner party or family gathering.

Ingredients:

- 4 boneless, skinless chicken breasts
- Salt and pepper, to taste
- 4 slices Swiss cheese
- 4 slices ham
- 1 cup all-purpose flour
- 2 large eggs, beaten
- 2 cups breadcrumbs
- 1 tablespoon vegetable oil
- 1 tablespoon butter
- For the Dijon Cream Sauce:
- 1/2 cup heavy cream
- 1 tablespoon Dijon mustard
- 1 teaspoon lemon juice
- Salt and pepper, to taste

Method:

1. Prepare the Chicken: Preheat your oven to 375°F (190°C). Butterfly each chicken breast, slicing it horizontally to open it like a book. Season with salt and pepper.

Place a slice of Swiss cheese and a slice of ham inside each chicken breast. Fold the chicken back over to close it.

2. Bread the Chicken: Dredge the stuffed chicken breasts in flour, dip them in beaten eggs, then coat in breadcrumbs.

3. Cook the Chicken: In a large skillet, heat oil and butter over medium heat. Cook the chicken for 4-5 minutes per side, until golden brown. Transfer the chicken to the oven and bake for 15-20 minutes, or until the chicken reaches an internal temperature of 165°F (74°C).

4. Make the Dijon Cream Sauce: In a small saucepan, combine heavy cream, Dijon mustard, and lemon juice. Bring to a simmer and cook for 3-4 minutes until thickened. Season with salt and pepper.

5. Serve: Drizzle the Dijon cream sauce over the chicken and serve with mashed potatoes or sautéed vegetables.

These Meat & Poultry recipes offer a range of flavors from different cultures and cooking methods, ensuring that your meals will be both exciting and satisfying. Whether you're grilling, roasting, or braising, these dishes will inspire you to explore new tastes and cooking techniques.

Chapter 6: Seafood Specialties – Celebrating the Ocean's Best

Seafood has always been celebrated for its fresh, delicate flavors, its versatility in the kitchen, and the immense variety it offers, from tender shellfish to meaty fish. As we delve into the world of seafood, we explore dishes that bring out the natural flavors of the ocean while incorporating unique techniques, spices, and textures. This chapter features 20 iconic seafood recipes, ranging from indulgent dishes like Lobster Mac and Cheese to light, flavorful plates such as Seared Scallops with Truffle Oil.

1. Black Rice Paella with Shellfish and Scallion Relish

Introduction: This Black Rice Paella is a twist on the classic Spanish dish, incorporating the deep, earthy tones of black rice. Combined with fresh shellfish, including shrimp, mussels, and clams, and topped with a refreshing scallion relish, this dish is as visually stunning as it is delicious.

Ingredients:

- 1 cup black rice
- 2 tablespoons olive oil
- 1 onion, chopped
- 2 cloves garlic, minced
- 1 red bell pepper, chopped
- 1/2 teaspoon saffron threads
- 1 cup dry white citrus
- 2 cups seafood stock
- 12 large shrimp, peeled and deveined
- 12 mussels, scrubbed
- 12 clams, scrubbed
- 1/2 cup frozen peas
- Salt and pepper, to taste
- For the Scallion Relish:
- 1/4 cup scallions, finely chopped
- 1 tablespoon lemon juice
- 1 teaspoon olive oil
- Salt and pepper, to taste

Method:

1. Prepare the Rice: Rinse the black rice under cold water until the water runs clear. Heat olive oil in a large paella pan over medium heat. Add the onion, garlic, and bell pepper, cooking until softened, about 5 minutes.
2. Cook the Paella Base: Stir in the saffron, followed by the white citrus, allowing it to cook for 2-3 minutes. Add the seafood stock and bring to a simmer. Add the black rice, cover, and reduce the heat to low. Let it cook for 30-40 minutes, or until the rice is tender.
3. Add Shellfish: Once the rice is cooked, gently stir in the shrimp, mussels, and clams, ensuring they are evenly distributed in the pan. Cover and cook for an additional 10 minutes, or until the shellfish have opened and the shrimp is cooked through.
4. Make the Relish: While the paella is cooking, combine scallions, lemon juice, olive oil, salt, and pepper in a small bowl.
5. Serve: Once the paella is ready, remove it from heat. Spoon the scallion relish over the top and serve with extra lemon wedges on the side.

---

2. Grilled Salmon with Lemon-Thyme Glaze

Introduction: This simple yet flavorful dish is a celebration of fresh salmon, enhanced by a zesty lemon-thyme glaze. The grill adds a smoky char, while the glaze infuses the fish with a refreshing citrus and herbaceous note.

Ingredients:

- 4 salmon fillets
- Salt and pepper, to taste
- 2 tablespoons olive oil
- 1/4 cup fresh lemon juice
- 2 teaspoons fresh thyme leaves
- 1 tablespoon honey
- 1 garlic clove, minced

Method:

1. Prepare the Salmon: Preheat your grill to medium-high heat. Season the salmon fillets with salt and pepper, and drizzle with olive oil.
2. Make the Lemon-Thyme Glaze: In a small saucepan, combine lemon juice, thyme, honey, and garlic. Simmer over medium heat for 5-7 minutes until the glaze has thickened slightly.
3. Grill the Salmon: Place the salmon fillets on the preheated grill, skin-side down. Grill for 4-5 minutes per side, or until the fish is cooked to your desired doneness.
4. Glaze the Fish: In the final minute of grilling, brush the salmon with the lemon-thyme glaze, allowing it to caramelize slightly.

5. Serve: Serve the salmon with a side of grilled vegetables or a fresh salad, and drizzle with extra glaze.

---

3. Shrimp Scampi with Garlic Butter

Introduction: Shrimp Scampi is a beloved Italian-American dish that's quick to prepare and full of flavor. The shrimp are sautéed in garlic-infused butter, white citrus, and a touch of lemon, making for a rich, garlicky sauce that pairs perfectly with pasta or crusty bread.

Ingredients:

- 1 lb large shrimp, peeled and deveined
- 3 tablespoons butter
- 4 cloves garlic, minced
- 1/2 cup dry white citrus
- 1 tablespoon fresh lemon juice
- 1/4 teaspoon red pepper flakes
- Salt and pepper, to taste
- 1/4 cup fresh parsley, chopped
- 1/2 lb linguine or spaghetti

Method:

1. Cook the Pasta: In a large pot of salted boiling water, cook the pasta according to the package instructions. Drain, reserving 1/4 cup of pasta water.
2. Cook the Shrimp: While the pasta cooks, melt butter in a large skillet over medium heat. Add the garlic and cook for 1 minute until fragrant. Add the shrimp to the skillet and sauté for 2-3 minutes until pink and cooked through.
3. Make the Sauce: Pour in the white citrus and lemon juice, scraping any brown bits from the bottom of the pan. Let the sauce simmer for 2 minutes, then add the red pepper flakes and season with salt and pepper.
4. Combine the Pasta and Shrimp: Add the drained pasta to the skillet, tossing to coat the pasta in the sauce. If the sauce is too thick, add a bit of reserved pasta water to loosen it.
5. Serve: Garnish with fresh parsley and serve immediately with extra lemon wedges and crusty bread.

4. Seared Scallops with Truffle Oil

Introduction: Seared Scallops are a luxurious dish that is surprisingly easy to prepare. The natural sweetness of the scallops is enhanced by a drizzle of fragrant truffle oil, making for an elegant appetizer or main course.

Ingredients:

- 12 large scallops, patted dry
- Salt and pepper, to taste
- 2 tablespoons olive oil
- 1 tablespoon unsalted butter
- 1 teaspoon truffle oil
- Fresh parsley, for garnish

Method:

1. Prepare the Scallops: Season the scallops with salt and pepper. Heat olive oil in a large skillet over high heat.
2. Sear the Scallops: Once the oil is hot, carefully place the scallops in the skillet, making sure not to overcrowd them. Sear for 2-3 minutes on each side until golden brown and cooked through.
3. Finish with Truffle Oil: Remove the scallops from the skillet and place them on a serving plate. Add butter to the skillet and let it melt. Drizzle in the truffle oil, stirring to combine.
4. Serve: Spoon the truffle butter over the scallops, garnish with fresh parsley, and serve with a light salad or roasted vegetables.

---

5. Lobster Mac and Cheese with a Crunchy Crust

Introduction: A decadent twist on the classic comfort food, Lobster Mac and Cheese combines rich, creamy cheese sauce with succulent lobster meat and a crispy breadcrumb topping. This dish is perfect for special occasions or an indulgent weeknight treat.

Ingredients:

- 1 lb elbow macaroni
- 2 lobster tails, cooked and chopped
- 4 tablespoons butter
- 1/4 cup all-purpose flour
- 2 cups whole milk

- 1 1/2 cups shredded cheddar cheese
- 1 cup shredded Gruyère cheese
- Salt and pepper, to taste
- 1/2 cup panko breadcrumbs
- 2 tablespoons melted butter

Method:

1. Cook the Pasta: Cook the macaroni in salted boiling water according to package instructions. Drain and set aside.
2. Make the Cheese Sauce: In a large saucepan, melt butter over medium heat. Whisk in flour and cook for 1 minute to form a roux. Gradually add the milk, whisking constantly, until the sauce thickens. Stir in the cheddar and Gruyère cheeses until melted. Season with salt and pepper.
3. Combine the Pasta and Lobster: Stir in the cooked macaroni and chopped lobster meat, mixing until well coated with the cheese sauce.
4. Prepare the Topping: In a small bowl, combine panko breadcrumbs with melted butter. Sprinkle the breadcrumbs evenly over the mac and cheese.
5. Bake: Transfer the mac and cheese to a greased baking dish and bake at 375°F (190°C) for 15-20 minutes, or until the top is golden and crispy.
6. Serve: Let cool for a few minutes before serving.

---

6. Cedar-Planked Salmon with Herb Butter

Introduction: Cedar-Planked Salmon is a show-stopping dish, where the fish is grilled on a cedar plank to infuse it with a smoky, woodsy flavor. Topped with a rich herb butter, this dish is perfect for a summer cookout or a special dinner.

Ingredients:

- 4 salmon fillets
- 1 cedar plank, soaked in water for at least 1 hour
- 2 tablespoons olive oil
- Salt and pepper, to taste
- For the Herb Butter:
- 1/4 cup unsalted butter, softened
- 1 tablespoon fresh parsley, chopped
- 1 teaspoon fresh dill, chopped
- 1 teaspoon lemon zest

Method:

1. Prepare the Cedar Plank: Preheat your grill to medium-high heat. Place the soaked cedar plank on the grill for 5-10 minutes to heat and create a smoky aroma.
2. Prepare the Salmon: Rub the salmon fillets with olive oil and season with salt and pepper.
3. Grill the Salmon: Place the salmon on the cedar plank and grill for 10-15 minutes, or until the fish flakes easily with a fork.
4. Make the Herb Butter: While the salmon grills, mix together the softened butter, parsley, dill, and lemon zest in a small bowl.
5. Serve: Once the salmon is cooked, remove it from the grill and spread the herb butter on top of each fillet. Serve immediately with your favorite side dishes.

7. Pan-Seared Red Snapper with Mango Salsa

Introduction: A light and refreshing dish, Pan-Seared Red Snapper pairs perfectly with a sweet and tangy Mango Salsa. The mild flavor of the snapper is enhanced by the vibrant and juicy salsa, creating a wonderful balance of flavors that transport you straight to the tropics.

Ingredients:

- 4 red snapper fillets, skin-on
- Salt and pepper, to taste
- 2 tablespoons olive oil
- 1 ripe mango, diced
- 1/4 cup red onion, finely chopped
- 1/4 cup cilantro, chopped
- 1 tablespoon lime juice
- 1 teaspoon jalapeño, finely chopped (optional)

Method:

1. Prepare the Salsa: In a bowl, combine the diced mango, red onion, cilantro, lime juice, and jalapeño (if using). Mix well and set aside.
2. Prepare the Snapper: Season the red snapper fillets with salt and pepper.
3. Pan-Sear the Fish: Heat olive oil in a large skillet over medium-high heat. Add the snapper fillets, skin-side down, and sear for 4-5 minutes on each side, until the fish is golden brown and cooked through.
4. Serve: Plate the fish and top with the mango salsa. Serve with rice or a light salad for a complete meal.

8. Mussels in White Citrus Garlic Sauce

Introduction: Mussels in White Citrus Garlic Sauce is an incredibly aromatic and flavorful dish. The briny mussels are cooked in a fragrant broth made with white citrus, garlic, and herbs, making this a perfect appetizer or main course served with a slice of crusty bread to soak up the delicious sauce.

Ingredients:

- 2 lbs fresh mussels, cleaned and debearded
- 2 tablespoons olive oil
- 4 cloves garlic, minced
- 1/2 cup dry white citrus
- 1/4 cup chicken or vegetable stock
- 2 tablespoons fresh parsley, chopped
- 1 tablespoon fresh thyme, chopped
- Salt and pepper, to taste
- Crusty bread, for serving

Method:

1. Prepare the Mussels: Rinse and scrub the mussels under cold water. Discard any that are cracked or do not close when tapped.
2. Cook the Garlic: Heat olive oil in a large pot over medium heat. Add the garlic and sauté for 1 minute, until fragrant.
3. Add Citrus and Stock: Pour in the white citrus and stock, bringing it to a simmer.
4. Cook the Mussels: Add the mussels to the pot and cover. Steam for 5-7 minutes, shaking the pot occasionally, until all the mussels have opened.
5. Finish the Dish: Remove from heat and stir in the fresh parsley and thyme. Season with salt and pepper to taste.
6. Serve: Serve the mussels with the broth and crusty bread on the side for dipping.

---

9. Cajun Blackened Catfish

Introduction: This Cajun Blackened Catfish is packed with bold flavors, thanks to a spicy Cajun seasoning blend. The catfish is pan-seared until crispy on the outside while remaining tender and juicy on the inside. This dish is perfect for those who enjoy a bit of heat in their meals.

Ingredients:

- 4 catfish fillets
- 2 tablespoons olive oil
- 2 teaspoons paprika
- 1 teaspoon garlic powder
- 1 teaspoon onion powder
- 1 teaspoon cayenne pepper
- 1 teaspoon dried thyme
- 1 teaspoon dried oregano
- Salt and pepper, to taste

Method:

1. Prepare the Seasoning: In a small bowl, combine paprika, garlic powder, onion powder, cayenne, thyme, oregano, salt, and pepper.
2. Season the Fish: Rub the catfish fillets with the seasoning blend, making sure each fillet is evenly coated.
3. Pan-Seer the Fish: Heat olive oil in a skillet over medium-high heat. Once hot, add the catfish fillets and cook for 3-4 minutes on each side, until crispy and golden brown.
4. Serve: Plate the blackened catfish and serve with a side of rice, roasted vegetables, or a crisp salad.

---

10. Coconut-Crusted Mahi-Mahi

Introduction: Coconut-Crusted Mahi-Mahi is a tropical dish with a crispy, golden coconut crust that perfectly complements the flaky fish. Served with a tangy dipping sauce or atop a bed of greens, this dish is a great way to enjoy mahi-mahi's mild flavor with a bit of sweet and savory crunch.

Ingredients:

- 4 mahi-mahi fillets
- 1/2 cup shredded coconut
- 1/2 cup panko breadcrumbs
- 1/4 cup flour
- 2 eggs, beaten
- Salt and pepper, to taste
- 2 tablespoons coconut oil

Method:

1. Prepare the Coating: In a shallow bowl, combine the shredded coconut, panko breadcrumbs, salt, and pepper.
2. Bread the Fish: Dredge each mahi-mahi fillet in flour, then dip in the beaten eggs, and finally coat with the coconut mixture, pressing gently to ensure the crust sticks.
3. Pan-Fry the Fish: Heat coconut oil in a large skillet over medium-high heat. Add the coated mahi-mahi fillets and cook for 3-4 minutes on each side, until golden brown and cooked through.
4. Serve: Serve the coconut-crusted mahi-mahi with a side of lime wedges and a simple dipping sauce like sweet chili or mango salsa.

---

11. Shrimp and Grits with Andouille Sausage

Introduction: Shrimp and Grits is a Southern classic that combines juicy shrimp with creamy, buttery grits. The addition of Andouille sausage brings a smoky, spicy flavor to this dish, making it hearty and satisfying, perfect for any meal of the day.

Ingredients:

- 1 lb large shrimp, peeled and deveined
- 2 tablespoons olive oil
- 2 Andouille sausage links, sliced
- 2 cloves garlic, minced
- 1 cup grits
- 4 cups water or chicken broth
- 1 cup heavy cream
- 1 tablespoon butter
- Salt and pepper, to taste
- 1 tablespoon fresh parsley, chopped

Method:

1. Cook the Grits: In a large saucepan, bring water or chicken broth to a boil. Stir in the grits, reduce the heat, and simmer, stirring occasionally, until thickened, about 15-20 minutes. Stir in the heavy cream, butter, salt, and pepper, and cook for another 5 minutes.
2. Cook the Sausage: While the grits cook, heat olive oil in a large skillet over medium heat. Add the sausage slices and cook until browned, about 4-5 minutes.
3. Cook the Shrimp: Add the garlic to the skillet and sauté for 1 minute. Add the shrimp and cook for 2-3 minutes on each side, until pink and cooked through.
4. Serve: Spoon the grits onto plates, top with the sausage and shrimp mixture, and garnish with fresh parsley. Serve hot.

12. Crab-Stuffed Mushrooms

Introduction: Crab-Stuffed Mushrooms are a delightful appetizer that features tender mushroom caps filled with a rich, savory crab filling. These bite-sized treats are perfect for any party or gathering, showcasing the sweetness of crab meat with a creamy, cheesy stuffing.

Ingredients:

- 12 large white mushrooms, stems removed
- 1/2 lb crab meat, drained and flaked
- 1/4 cup cream cheese, softened
- 1/4 cup Parmesan cheese, grated
- 1/4 cup breadcrumbs
- 2 tablespoons fresh parsley, chopped
- 1 teaspoon garlic powder
- Salt and pepper, to taste
- 1 tablespoon butter, melted

Method:

1. Prepare the Mushrooms: Preheat the oven to 375°F (190°C). Arrange the mushroom caps on a baking sheet, gill-side up.
2. Make the Stuffing: In a bowl, combine crab meat, cream cheese, Parmesan cheese, breadcrumbs, parsley, garlic powder, salt, and pepper. Mix until well combined.
3. Stuff the Mushrooms: Spoon the crab mixture into each mushroom cap, pressing it down gently to fill them.
4. Bake: Drizzle melted butter over the stuffed mushrooms and bake for 15-20 minutes, or until the mushrooms are tender and the stuffing is golden brown.
5. Serve: Serve immediately as an appetizer or part of a larger seafood feast.

13. Clams Casino

Introduction: A true classic, Clams Casino brings together tender clams with a crispy, savory topping of bacon, breadcrumbs, and Parmesan cheese. This dish is an iconic seafood appetizer, perfect for any special occasion, but also easy enough to make as a treat for a weekend dinner.

Ingredients:

- 12 fresh clams, shucked, keeping the shells
- 4 slices bacon, chopped
- 1/2 cup breadcrumbs
- 1/4 cup grated Parmesan cheese
- 2 tablespoons fresh parsley, chopped
- 1 clove garlic, minced
- 1 tablespoon butter
- 1 tablespoon olive oil
- 1 teaspoon lemon juice
- Salt and pepper, to taste

Method:

1. Prepare the Clams: Preheat the oven to 375°F (190°C). Shuck the clams, keeping them in their shells. Arrange the clam shells on a baking dish.
2. Cook the Bacon: In a skillet over medium heat, cook the chopped bacon until crispy, about 4-5 minutes. Remove the bacon from the pan and set aside. Leave the bacon drippings in the pan.
3. Make the Topping: In the same skillet, add the butter and olive oil, followed by the garlic. Sauté for about 1 minute until fragrant. Add the breadcrumbs and cook for an additional 2-3 minutes until golden brown. Stir in the Parmesan cheese, bacon, parsley, and a squeeze of lemon juice. Season with salt and pepper.
4. Stuff the Clams: Spoon the breadcrumb mixture into each clam shell, making sure to pack it tightly.
5. Bake the Clams: Place the stuffed clams in the oven and bake for 10-12 minutes, or until the topping is golden and crispy.
6. Serve: Serve the clams immediately with a wedge of lemon for added freshness.

---

14. Grilled Oysters with Herb Butter

Introduction: Grilled Oysters with Herb Butter brings together the delicate brininess of oysters and the rich, herby goodness of garlic butter. When grilled, oysters absorb a lovely smoky flavor while the butter melts into the oyster's flesh, creating a succulent bite that's sure to impress.

Ingredients:

- 12 oysters, shucked and on the half shell
- 1/2 cup unsalted butter, softened
- 2 cloves garlic, minced
- 1 tablespoon fresh parsley, chopped

- 1 teaspoon fresh thyme, chopped
- 1 teaspoon lemon zest
- 1 tablespoon lemon juice
- Salt and pepper, to taste

1 tablespoon grated Parmesan cheese (optional)

Method:

1. Prepare the Herb Butter: In a bowl, combine softened butter, garlic, parsley, thyme, lemon zest, and lemon juice. Season with salt and pepper, and stir well to combine.
2. Prepare the Oysters: Preheat your grill to medium-high heat. Place the oysters on the grill, with the cupped side down to hold the oyster's juices.
3. Top the Oysters: Spoon about a teaspoon of the herb butter mixture onto each oyster.
4. Grill the Oysters: Close the grill lid and cook the oysters for 5-7 minutes, or until the oysters are hot and the butter has melted into the oysters.
5. Finish and Serve: Optional: Sprinkle a little Parmesan cheese on top of each oyster and return them to the grill for another 1-2 minutes. Remove from the grill and serve immediately with extra lemon wedges.

---

15. Yellowfin Tuna Steak with Wasabi Aioli

Introduction: Yellowfin Tuna Steak is a simple yet elegant dish that is seared to perfection and paired with a creamy Wasabi Aioli for a punch of flavor. The aioli adds a spicy, tangy kick that complements the tender tuna, making for an unforgettable meal.

Ingredients:

- 2 tuna steaks (about 6 oz each)
- 2 tablespoons olive oil
- Salt and pepper, to taste
- 1/2 cup mayonnaise
- 1 tablespoon wasabi paste (or more, to taste)
- 1 teaspoon soy sauce
- 1 teaspoon lemon juice
- 1 tablespoon sesame seeds (optional)

Method:

1. Prepare the Wasabi Aioli: In a small bowl, whisk together the mayonnaise, wasabi paste, soy sauce, and lemon juice until smooth. Adjust the level of wasabi to your preference for heat.
2. Season the Tuna: Rub the tuna steaks with olive oil and season generously with salt and pepper.
3. Sear the Tuna: Heat a non-stick skillet or grill pan over medium-high heat. Sear the tuna steaks for 1-2 minutes on each side for rare, or cook longer if you prefer it more done. Be careful not to overcook the tuna, as it's best served rare to medium-rare.
4. Serve: Plate the tuna steaks and drizzle with wasabi aioli. Sprinkle sesame seeds on top for an added crunch. Serve with a side of rice or a fresh salad.

---

16. Fried Soft-Shell Crab Sandwiches

Introduction: Fried Soft-Shell Crab Sandwiches are a true summer indulgence. The soft-shell crabs are battered and fried until crispy, then tucked into a soft bun with a zesty slaw. The combination of crispy crab and tangy slaw creates a sensational sandwich that's perfect for a casual gathering.

Ingredients:

- 4 soft-shell crabs, cleaned and prepped
- 1 cup all-purpose flour
- 1/2 cup cornmeal
- 1 teaspoon paprika
- Salt and pepper, to taste
- 2 eggs, beaten
- Vegetable oil, for frying
- 4 soft sandwich rolls or brioche buns
- 1/2 cup coleslaw (store-bought or homemade)
- Lemon wedges, for serving

Method:

1. Prepare the Crab: Pat the soft-shell crabs dry with paper towels. In a shallow dish, combine the flour, cornmeal, paprika, salt, and pepper.
2. Batter the Crabs: Dip each crab in the beaten eggs, then dredge in the flour mixture, pressing gently to ensure it sticks.
3. Fry the Crabs: Heat vegetable oil in a deep pan over medium-high heat. Fry the crabs for 3-4 minutes on each side, until golden and crispy. Remove from the oil and drain on paper towels.

4. Assemble the Sandwiches: Toast the sandwich rolls lightly, then spread a little mayonnaise or tartar sauce on the bottom of each roll. Top with a fried crab, followed by a spoonful of coleslaw.
5. Serve: Serve the sandwiches with lemon wedges on the side for extra brightness.

---

17. Baked Cod with Lemon and Dill

Introduction: A simple yet delicious dish, Baked Cod with Lemon and Dill is light, fresh, and full of flavor. The cod is gently baked in the oven with a drizzle of lemon and a sprinkle of dill, allowing the natural sweetness of the fish to shine.

Ingredients:

- 4 cod fillets (6 oz each)
- 2 tablespoons olive oil
- 1 lemon, thinly sliced
- 1 tablespoon fresh dill, chopped
- Salt and pepper, to taste
- 1 tablespoon butter, optional

Method:

1. Prepare the Cod: Preheat your oven to 375°F (190°C). Place the cod fillets on a baking sheet lined with parchment paper.
2. Season the Fish: Drizzle the olive oil over the cod fillets and season with salt and pepper. Place lemon slices on top of each fillet, then sprinkle with fresh dill.
3. Bake the Cod: Bake the fish for 12-15 minutes, or until it flakes easily with a fork. If desired, you can place a small pat of butter on top of each fillet for added richness.
4. Serve: Plate the baked cod and serve with additional lemon wedges for squeezing over the fish. This pairs wonderfully with steamed vegetables or a light salad.

---

18. Bouillabaisse (French Fisherman's Stew)

Introduction: Bouillabaisse is a traditional French seafood stew made with a variety of fresh fish and shellfish, cooked with aromatic vegetables and herbs in a rich, savory broth. This dish is perfect for showcasing an array of seafood and is ideal for sharing with friends and family.

Ingredients:

- 1 lb white fish (such as cod, halibut, or snapper), cut into chunks
- 1 lb shellfish (mussels, clams, or shrimp), cleaned and deveined
- 1/2 cup olive oil
- 1 onion, chopped
- 2 leeks, white and light green parts only, sliced
- 2 cloves garlic, minced
- 2 tomatoes, chopped
- 4 cups fish stock or broth
- 1 cup dry white citrus
- 1 teaspoon saffron threads
- 1 bay leaf
- 1 teaspoon fresh thyme
- Salt and pepper, to taste
- Fresh parsley, chopped, for garnish

Method:

1. Prepare the Broth: In a large pot, heat olive oil over medium heat. Add the onion, leeks, and garlic, and sauté for 5-7 minutes until softened.
2. Add Tomatoes and Broth: Stir in the tomatoes, then add the fish stock, white citrus, saffron, bay leaf, thyme, salt, and pepper. Bring to a simmer and cook for 20 minutes.
3. Add the Fish and Shellfish: Add the white fish and shellfish to the pot. Simmer for an additional 10-12 minutes, or until the fish is cooked through and the shellfish has opened.
4. Serve: Ladle the bouillabaisse into bowls and garnish with fresh parsley. Serve with crusty French bread and a dollop of rouille (garlic mayonnaise) on the side.

---

19. Grilled Swordfish with Tomato Basil Salsa

Introduction: Grilled swordfish is a firm, meaty fish that holds up beautifully on the grill. Paired with a fresh, tangy tomato basil salsa, this dish offers a perfect balance of smoky, savory, and bright flavors. It's ideal for summer barbecues or an elegant dinner.

Ingredients:

- 4 swordfish steaks (about 6 oz each)
- 2 tablespoons olive oil
- Salt and pepper, to taste
- 2 large tomatoes, diced
- 1/4 cup fresh basil, chopped
- 1 tablespoon red onion, finely diced

- 1 tablespoon balsamic vinegar
- 1 teaspoon olive oil
- 1 teaspoon lemon juice

Method:

1. Prepare the Swordfish: Preheat the grill to medium-high heat. Brush the swordfish steaks with olive oil and season with salt and pepper on both sides.
2. Grill the Swordfish: Place the swordfish on the grill and cook for about 3-4 minutes per side, depending on thickness, until it has grill marks and is cooked through but still moist.
3. Make the Salsa: While the swordfish is grilling, combine the diced tomatoes, basil, red onion, balsamic vinegar, olive oil, and lemon juice in a small bowl. Stir well and season with salt and pepper to taste.
4. Serve: Once the swordfish is cooked, plate it and top with the fresh tomato basil salsa. Serve with grilled vegetables or a light salad on the side.

---

20. Lobster Rolls with Lemon Mayo

Introduction: There's nothing quite as indulgent and satisfying as a Lobster Roll. Sweet lobster meat is dressed with a light lemon mayo and tucked into a soft, toasted roll for a truly classic New England experience. Perfect for summer lunches or a special dinner.

Ingredients:

- 2 lobster tails, cooked and chopped (or 1 lb cooked lobster meat)
- 2 tablespoons mayonnaise
- 1 tablespoon lemon juice
- 1 teaspoon lemon zest
- 1 tablespoon fresh chives, chopped
- Salt and pepper, to taste
- 4 New England-style rolls (split-top rolls)
- 2 tablespoons butter, melted

Method:

1. Prepare the Lobster: If using lobster tails, boil or steam them until cooked through, about 5-6 minutes. Let them cool slightly, then chop the meat into bite-sized pieces.
2. Make the Lemon Mayo: In a small bowl, combine mayonnaise, lemon juice, lemon zest, fresh chives, salt, and pepper. Stir until smooth.
3. Assemble the Rolls: Heat a skillet over medium heat and brush the rolls with melted butter. Toast them in the skillet until golden brown and crispy.

4. Fill the Rolls: Once the rolls are toasted, fill each one with the chopped lobster meat. Spoon a generous amount of lemon mayo over the lobster.
5. Serve: Serve the lobster rolls immediately with a side of coleslaw or crispy fries.

Conclusion of the Chapter:

In this chapter, you've explored the variety and versatility of seafood, from simple grilled fish to indulgent lobster rolls. Whether you're preparing a light, fresh salad with shrimp or a hearty fish stew, seafood offers endless opportunities for creativity in the kitchen. The key to successful seafood dishes lies in using the freshest ingredients, enhancing their natural flavors, and pairing them with complementary ingredients that elevate the dish.

Remember, cooking seafood doesn't have to be intimidating. With the right techniques and a few key ingredients, you can create memorable meals that celebrate the flavors of the ocean. Keep experimenting with different spices, sauces, and cooking methods—whether grilling, baking, or sautéing—and enjoy bringing these delicious dishes to your table!

These recipes offer a great starting point for anyone interested in exploring the world of seafood cooking, inspired by Bobby Flay's flavor-forward approach to food. Whether you're a beginner or an experienced chef, the techniques and flavor profiles in this chapter will guide you in crafting exceptional seafood dishes that shine with every bite.

7. Vegetarian and Plant-Based Dishes (20 Recipes)

Exploring Plant-Based Ingredients and Techniques

The world of vegetarian and plant-based cooking offers an abundance of flavors, textures, and colors that can be as satisfying, if not more so, than traditional meat-based dishes. These recipes showcase a variety of plant-based ingredients, such as vibrant vegetables, hearty legumes, wholesome grains, and aromatic herbs, combined with different cooking techniques to create dishes that are not only nourishing but bursting with flavor.

Plant-based cooking often invites creativity, as it allows the chef to experiment with the natural sweetness, earthiness, and complexity of fresh produce. From hearty stews to refreshing salads, and from roasted vegetables to creamy pasta alternatives, plant-based cooking is all about letting the ingredients shine. Through careful seasoning and thoughtful techniques, plant-based meals can offer satisfying textures, rich flavors, and comforting bites that leave a lasting impression.

In this chapter, you'll find recipes that demonstrate the versatility of vegetables and plant-based foods, turning them into unforgettable main dishes that are both wholesome and flavorful. Whether you're a dedicated vegetarian, a flexitarian, or just looking to explore new plant-based meals, these recipes provide a wonderful way to incorporate more plant-based ingredients into your cooking.

1. Spiced Cauliflower Steak with Chimichurri

Introduction: Cauliflower is one of the most versatile vegetables, and when prepared as a "steak," it becomes a satisfying, meaty alternative to traditional grilled cuts. The Spiced Cauliflower Steak with Chimichurri offers bold flavors with a perfect balance of smoky, spicy, and tangy notes. The chimichurri sauce, made with fresh herbs and tangy vinegar, complements the roasted cauliflower beautifully.

Ingredients:

- 1 large head of cauliflower
- 2 tablespoons olive oil
- 1 teaspoon ground cumin
- 1 teaspoon paprika
- 1/2 teaspoon garlic powder

- Salt and pepper, to taste
- Fresh parsley for garnish
- For the Chimichurri:
- 1 cup fresh parsley, chopped
- 3 tablespoons red citrus vinegar
- 2 cloves garlic, minced
- 1/2 teaspoon red pepper flakes
- 1/4 cup olive oil
- Salt and pepper, to taste

Method:

1. Prepare the Cauliflower Steaks: Preheat the oven to 400°F (200°C). Remove the outer leaves from the cauliflower and slice it into 3/4-inch-thick steaks, keeping the core intact to hold the slices together.
2. Season the Cauliflower: In a small bowl, mix the olive oil, cumin, paprika, garlic powder, salt, and pepper. Brush both sides of the cauliflower steaks with the spice mixture.
3. Roast the Cauliflower: Place the cauliflower steaks on a baking sheet and roast for 20-25 minutes, flipping halfway through, until tender and golden brown on the edges.
4. Make the Chimichurri: While the cauliflower is roasting, combine all the chimichurri ingredients in a bowl. Stir well and let sit for 10 minutes to allow the flavors to meld.
5. Serve: Once the cauliflower steaks are done, drizzle with chimichurri sauce and garnish with fresh parsley. Serve immediately with a side of quinoa or rice.

---

2. Grilled Portobello Mushroom Burgers

Introduction: Portobello mushrooms are the perfect substitute for meat in burgers, thanks to their meaty texture and umami flavor. These Grilled Portobello Mushroom Burgers are juicy, tender, and packed with flavor, while the addition of tangy toppings and a soft, toasted bun makes for a satisfying plant-based meal.

Ingredients:

- 4 large Portobello mushroom caps, stems removed
- 2 tablespoons balsamic vinegar
- 2 tablespoons olive oil
- 1 teaspoon garlic powder
- Salt and pepper, to taste
- 4 burger buns

- 1/2 cup lettuce, shredded
- 1 tomato, sliced
- 1/4 cup vegan mayonnaise or aioli
- 1 tablespoon Dijon mustard
- 1 tablespoon fresh basil, chopped (optional)

Method:

1. Marinate the Mushrooms: In a small bowl, whisk together balsamic vinegar, olive oil, garlic powder, salt, and pepper. Brush both sides of the mushroom caps with the marinade and let sit for at least 15 minutes.
2. Grill the Mushrooms: Preheat a grill or grill pan to medium heat. Grill the mushrooms for about 5-7 minutes on each side, until they are tender and have nice grill marks.
3. Toast the Buns: While the mushrooms are grilling, toast the burger buns on the grill for 1-2 minutes until lightly crispy.
4. Assemble the Burgers: Spread vegan mayonnaise or aioli on the bottom half of each toasted bun. Place a grilled Portobello mushroom on top, followed by a slice of tomato, shredded lettuce, and a dollop of Dijon mustard. Garnish with fresh basil if desired.
5. Serve: Serve the burgers with a side of crispy sweet potato fries or a simple salad.

---

3. Ratatouille with Fresh Herbs

Introduction: A quintessential French dish, Ratatouille is a vibrant vegetable stew featuring eggplant, zucchini, peppers, and tomatoes, simmered in olive oil with fragrant herbs. This dish is a celebration of summer produce and offers rich, comforting flavors while being completely plant-based.

Ingredients:

- 1 eggplant, diced
- 2 zucchini, sliced
- 1 bell pepper, chopped
- 1 onion, chopped
- 3 tomatoes, chopped
- 2 cloves garlic, minced
- 2 tablespoons olive oil
- 1 teaspoon dried thyme
- 1 teaspoon dried oregano
- Fresh basil leaves, chopped (for garnish)

- Salt and pepper, to taste

Method:

1. Sauté the Vegetables: In a large skillet, heat the olive oil over medium heat. Add the onion and garlic, sautéing until softened, about 5 minutes. Add the bell pepper and cook for another 5 minutes.
2. Add the Remaining Vegetables: Add the diced eggplant and zucchini, and cook for 10 minutes, stirring occasionally, until the vegetables begin to soften.
3. Simmer the Stew: Add the chopped tomatoes, thyme, oregano, salt, and pepper to the skillet. Stir well and simmer for 15-20 minutes, or until the vegetables are tender and the flavors have melded together.
4. Serve: Garnish with fresh basil and serve the ratatouille with crusty bread or over couscous.

4. Eggplant Parmesan with Tomato Basil Sauce

Introduction: Eggplant Parmesan is a beloved Italian classic, and this plant-based version is just as indulgent and flavorful. Layers of crispy breaded eggplant are smothered in a rich tomato basil sauce and topped with a melty vegan cheese for a comforting, satisfying meal.

Ingredients:

- 2 medium eggplants, sliced into 1/2-inch rounds
- 1 cup breadcrumbs (use gluten-free if needed)
- 1/2 cup all-purpose flour
- 1/2 cup non-dairy milk
- Salt and pepper, to taste
- 2 cups marinara sauce
- 1/2 cup fresh basil, chopped
- 1 cup vegan mozzarella cheese, shredded
- Olive oil, for frying

Method:

1. Prepare the Eggplant: Preheat the oven to 375°F (190°C). Arrange the eggplant slices on a paper towel and sprinkle with salt. Let them sit for 15 minutes to draw out excess moisture.
2. Bread the Eggplant: In one bowl, place the flour. In another, pour the non-dairy milk. In a third bowl, place the breadcrumbs. Dredge each eggplant slice in flour, dip in milk, and coat with breadcrumbs.

3. Fry the Eggplant: Heat a few tablespoons of olive oil in a skillet over medium heat. Fry the breaded eggplant slices for 2-3 minutes on each side, until golden brown and crispy. Remove and set aside on a paper towel.
4. Assemble the Parmesan: In a baking dish, spread a thin layer of marinara sauce. Layer the fried eggplant slices on top, followed by more marinara sauce, fresh basil, and a sprinkle of vegan mozzarella. Repeat the layers until all ingredients are used.
5. Bake: Bake in the preheated oven for 20-25 minutes, or until the cheese is melted and bubbly.
6. Serve: Garnish with extra fresh basil and serve with pasta or a simple green salad.

---

5. Roasted Vegetable Paella with Saffron

Introduction: Paella is a Spanish rice dish typically made with seafood or meats, but this plant-based version focuses on the vibrant flavors of roasted vegetables and aromatic saffron. The dish is as rich in color as it is in flavor, offering a satisfying, hearty meal that's ideal for family dinners or dinner parties.

Ingredients:

- 1 red bell pepper, sliced
- 1 yellow bell pepper, sliced
- 1 small zucchini, chopped
- 1 eggplant, chopped
- 1 onion, sliced
- 1 cup Arborio rice
- 2 cups vegetable broth
- 1 teaspoon saffron threads
- 2 cloves garlic, minced
- 1 teaspoon smoked paprika
- 1 teaspoon turmeric
- Olive oil, for roasting
- Salt and pepper, to taste
- Fresh parsley for garnish

Method:

1. Roast the Vegetables: Preheat the oven to 400°F (200°C). Arrange the bell peppers, zucchini, eggplant, and onion on a baking sheet. Drizzle with olive oil, season with salt and pepper, and roast for 20-25 minutes, or until the vegetables are tender.

2. Prepare the Paella Base: In a large pan, heat a tablespoon of olive oil over medium heat. Add the garlic, smoked paprika, and turmeric. Sauté for 1-2 minutes until fragrant.
3. Cook the Rice: Add the Arborio rice to the pan and stir for 1-2 minutes to coat the rice in the spices. Add the vegetable broth and saffron threads, bring to a simmer, and cook for about 15 minutes, until the rice is tender and the liquid has been absorbed.
4. Combine and Serve: Gently stir in the roasted vegetables and cook for another 5 minutes to heat through. Garnish with fresh parsley before serving.

6. Butternut Squash and Kale Lasagna

Introduction: A plant-based twist on a classic Italian favorite, Butternut Squash and Kale Lasagna is a rich and satisfying dish that combines the sweetness of roasted butternut squash, the earthiness of kale, and layers of creamy, plant-based ricotta. Perfect for family dinners or gatherings, this lasagna is comforting, nourishing, and sure to impress.

Ingredients:

- 12 lasagna noodles (whole wheat or gluten-free)
- 1 small butternut squash, peeled and diced
- 2 tablespoons olive oil
- Salt and pepper, to taste
- 3 cups kale, chopped
- 2 cups vegan ricotta cheese (store-bought or homemade)
- 1/2 cup nutritional yeast
- 2 cups marinara sauce
- 1 teaspoon garlic powder
- Fresh basil leaves, for garnish

Method:

1. Roast the Butternut Squash: Preheat the oven to 400°F (200°C). Toss the butternut squash with olive oil, salt, and pepper. Roast on a baking sheet for 25-30 minutes, or until tender and lightly browned.
2. Prepare the Kale: In a large skillet, sauté the kale over medium heat with a bit of olive oil for about 5-7 minutes, until wilted and tender. Season with salt and pepper.
3. Cook the Lasagna Noodles: Cook the lasagna noodles according to package instructions. Drain and set aside.
4. Assemble the Lasagna: In a baking dish, spread a thin layer of marinara sauce. Layer with lasagna noodles, followed by roasted butternut squash, sautéed kale, a layer of vegan ricotta cheese, and a sprinkle of nutritional yeast. Repeat the layers until all

ingredients are used, finishing with a layer of marinara sauce and a sprinkle of nutritional yeast on top.

5. Bake: Cover with foil and bake at 375°F (190°C) for 35-40 minutes. Remove the foil and bake for an additional 10 minutes to brown the top.
6. Serve: Let the lasagna cool for a few minutes before slicing. Garnish with fresh basil and serve with a side salad.

---

7. Chickpea and Sweet Potato Curry

Introduction: This Chickpea and Sweet Potato Curry is a hearty and flavorful dish with the warmth of curry spices and the sweetness of roasted sweet potatoes. The chickpeas add protein and texture, while coconut milk brings richness and creaminess. This dish is perfect over a bed of rice or with naan for a complete meal.

Ingredients:

- 1 large sweet potato, peeled and diced
- 1 tablespoon olive oil
- Salt and pepper, to taste
- 1 onion, diced
- 2 cloves garlic, minced
- 1 tablespoon fresh ginger, grated
- 1 tablespoon curry powder
- 1 teaspoon ground cumin
- 1 teaspoon turmeric
- 1 can (15 oz) chickpeas, drained and rinsed
- 1 can (14 oz) coconut milk
- 1 cup vegetable broth
- 2 cups spinach, chopped
- Fresh cilantro, for garnish

Method:

1. Roast the Sweet Potatoes: Preheat the oven to 400°F (200°C). Toss the sweet potato cubes with olive oil, salt, and pepper. Spread them on a baking sheet and roast for 20-25 minutes, or until tender.
2. Prepare the Curry Base: In a large pot, heat olive oil over medium heat. Add the onion, garlic, and ginger and sauté for 5 minutes until softened. Stir in the curry powder, cumin, and turmeric and cook for 1-2 minutes to bloom the spices.

3. Simmer the Curry: Add the chickpeas, coconut milk, vegetable broth, and roasted sweet potatoes to the pot. Bring to a simmer and cook for 10-15 minutes to allow the flavors to meld together.
4. Finish the Curry: Stir in the spinach and cook for another 2-3 minutes until wilted. Adjust seasoning with salt and pepper as needed.
5. Serve: Ladle the curry over rice or serve with naan. Garnish with fresh cilantro before serving.

---

8. Stuffed Bell Peppers with Quinoa

Introduction: Stuffed Bell Peppers with Quinoa are a hearty and nutritious meal, perfect for a weeknight dinner. Quinoa is a complete protein, and when combined with vegetables, herbs, and spices, it makes a filling and delicious stuffing for vibrant bell peppers. These peppers are baked until tender and offer a satisfying, colorful meal.

Ingredients:

- 4 bell peppers, tops cut off and seeds removed
- 1 cup quinoa, rinsed
- 2 cups vegetable broth
- 1 can (15 oz) black beans, drained and rinsed
- 1 cup corn kernels (fresh, frozen, or canned)
- 1 tablespoon olive oil
- 1 teaspoon cumin
- 1 teaspoon chili powder
- 1/2 teaspoon paprika
- 1/4 cup fresh cilantro, chopped
- Salt and pepper, to taste
- 1/2 cup vegan cheese (optional)

Method:

1. Cook the Quinoa: In a medium saucepan, bring the vegetable broth to a boil. Add the quinoa, reduce the heat to low, and cover. Cook for 15 minutes, or until the quinoa is tender and the liquid is absorbed. Fluff with a fork.
2. Prepare the Filling: In a large bowl, combine the cooked quinoa, black beans, corn, olive oil, cumin, chili powder, paprika, cilantro, salt, and pepper. Stir well to combine.
3. Stuff the Peppers: Preheat the oven to 375°F (190°C). Stuff each bell pepper with the quinoa mixture, packing it tightly. Place the stuffed peppers in a baking dish.
4. Bake: Cover with foil and bake for 25-30 minutes, until the peppers are tender. If using vegan cheese, sprinkle it on top during the last 5 minutes of baking.

5. Serve: Serve the stuffed peppers with a side salad or roasted vegetables.

---

9. Black Bean and Corn Tacos with Avocado

Introduction: These Black Bean and Corn Tacos with Avocado are a quick and flavorful weeknight dinner that brings together the hearty goodness of black beans, the sweetness of corn, and the creaminess of avocado, all wrapped in a warm tortilla. These tacos are easy to make and packed with vibrant flavors.

Ingredients:

- 1 can (15 oz) black beans, drained and rinsed
- 1 cup corn kernels (fresh, frozen, or canned)
- 1 tablespoon olive oil
- 1 teaspoon cumin
- 1 teaspoon chili powder
- 1/2 teaspoon garlic powder
- Salt and pepper, to taste
- 8 small corn tortillas
- 1 avocado, sliced
- Fresh cilantro, for garnish
- Lime wedges, for serving

Method:

1. Prepare the Filling: In a large skillet, heat the olive oil over medium heat. Add the black beans and corn. Season with cumin, chili powder, garlic powder, salt, and pepper. Cook for 5-7 minutes, stirring occasionally, until heated through.
2. Warm the Tortillas: Heat the tortillas on a dry skillet over medium heat for about 30 seconds per side until warm and slightly crispy.
3. Assemble the Tacos: Spoon the black bean and corn mixture onto each tortilla. Top with sliced avocado, fresh cilantro, and a squeeze of lime juice.
4. Serve: Serve the tacos immediately with extra lime wedges and a side of salsa or guacamole.

---

10. Grilled Halloumi with Watermelon Salad

Introduction: Grilled Halloumi with Watermelon Salad is a refreshing and light dish that combines the savory, slightly salty flavor of grilled Halloumi cheese with the sweetness of fresh watermelon. This dish is perfect for summer and is great as an appetizer or light main course.

Ingredients:

- 8 oz Halloumi cheese, sliced into 1/2-inch thick slices
- 2 cups watermelon, diced
- 1/2 cucumber, thinly sliced
- 1/4 red onion, thinly sliced
- 1 tablespoon fresh mint, chopped
- 1 tablespoon olive oil
- Salt and pepper, to taste
- Juice of 1 lime

Method:

1. Grill the Halloumi: Preheat the grill or grill pan over medium heat. Grill the Halloumi slices for 2-3 minutes on each side until golden brown and slightly crispy.
2. Prepare the Salad: In a large bowl, combine the diced watermelon, cucumber, red onion, and mint. Drizzle with olive oil and lime juice. Season with salt and pepper to taste.
3. Serve: Plate the salad and top with the grilled Halloumi slices. Serve immediately as a refreshing, light dish.

11. Zucchini Noodles with Pesto

Introduction: Zucchini Noodles with Pesto offer a fresh, low-carb twist on a classic pasta dish. The zucchini noodles provide a satisfying crunch, and the vibrant, fragrant pesto sauce brings all the flavors together. This dish is light, yet filling, and a great way to incorporate more vegetables into your diet.

Ingredients:

- 4 medium zucchini, spiralized into noodles
- 1 cup fresh basil leaves
- 1/4 cup pine nuts (or walnuts)
- 2 cloves garlic
- 1/4 cup nutritional yeast (or Parmesan if not vegan)
- 1/2 cup extra virgin olive oil
- Juice of 1/2 lemon
- Salt and pepper, to taste
- Cherry tomatoes, for garnish (optional)

Method:

1. Make the Pesto: In a food processor, combine the basil, pine nuts, garlic, nutritional yeast, lemon juice, salt, and pepper. Pulse until everything is finely chopped. With the food processor running, slowly stream in the olive oil until the pesto reaches a smooth consistency.
2. Prepare the Zucchini Noodles: If you don't already have pre-spiralized zucchini, use a spiralizer to make zucchini noodles. You can also use a vegetable peeler to create ribbons if needed.
3. Toss and Serve: Heat a large pan over medium heat. Add the zucchini noodles and sauté for 2-3 minutes until just tender. Remove from heat and toss with the pesto sauce.
4. Garnish and Serve: Top with halved cherry tomatoes for added color and flavor. Serve immediately.

12. Moroccan Vegetable Tagine

Introduction: A Moroccan Vegetable Tagine is a rich and aromatic stew that showcases the warm spices of North Africa. The vegetables are slow-cooked in a fragrant broth infused with cumin, cinnamon, turmeric, and saffron, creating a dish that's hearty, flavorful, and full of complex tastes. Served over couscous, it's a comforting, vibrant meal.

Ingredients:

- 1 tablespoon olive oil
- 1 onion, chopped
- 2 cloves garlic, minced
- 2 carrots, peeled and diced
- 1 zucchini, chopped
- 1 bell pepper, chopped
- 1 sweet potato, peeled and cubed
- 1 can (15 oz) chickpeas, drained and rinsed
- 1 can (14 oz) diced tomatoes
- 1/2 cup dried apricots, chopped
- 1 teaspoon cumin
- 1 teaspoon cinnamon
- 1 teaspoon turmeric
- 1/2 teaspoon ground ginger
- 1/4 teaspoon saffron threads (optional)
- 2 cups vegetable broth
- Salt and pepper, to taste
- Fresh cilantro, chopped, for garnish

- Couscous or rice, for serving

Method:

1. Sauté the Vegetables: Heat olive oil in a large pot or tagine over medium heat. Add the onion and garlic and cook for 3-4 minutes, until softened. Add the carrots, zucchini, bell pepper, and sweet potato and cook for another 5 minutes, stirring occasionally.
2. Add Spices and Simmer: Stir in the cumin, cinnamon, turmeric, ginger, saffron, salt, and pepper. Add the chickpeas, tomatoes, apricots, and vegetable broth. Bring to a simmer and cook for 30-40 minutes, until the vegetables are tender and the flavors meld.
3. Serve: Serve the tagine over couscous or rice. Garnish with fresh cilantro before serving.

---

13. Lentil Shepherd's Pie

Introduction: This Lentil Shepherd's Pie is a hearty, vegan version of the classic British comfort food. The lentils, cooked in a rich tomato and vegetable sauce, are topped with creamy mashed potatoes and baked until golden brown. It's a filling, flavorful dish that's perfect for a family meal or a cozy dinner.

Ingredients:

- 2 cups green or brown lentils
- 1 tablespoon olive oil
- 1 onion, chopped
- 2 cloves garlic, minced
- 2 carrots, diced
- 1 cup frozen peas
- 2 tablespoons tomato paste
- 1 can (14 oz) diced tomatoes
- 2 teaspoons dried thyme
- 1 teaspoon paprika
- Salt and pepper, to taste
- 4 large potatoes, peeled and diced
- 1/4 cup unsweetened almond milk (or regular milk)
- 2 tablespoons vegan butter (or regular butter)
- Fresh parsley, chopped, for garnish

Method:

1. Prepare the Lentil Filling: Cook the lentils according to package instructions. In a large skillet, heat olive oil over medium heat. Add the onion and garlic and sauté for 3-4 minutes. Add the carrots, peas, tomato paste, diced tomatoes, thyme, paprika, salt, and pepper. Stir in the cooked lentils and simmer for 15-20 minutes, until the mixture thickens.
2. Make the Mashed Potatoes: Meanwhile, cook the potatoes in a large pot of boiling salted water until tender, about 15-20 minutes. Drain and mash with almond milk, butter, salt, and pepper until smooth and creamy.
3. Assemble the Shepherd's Pie: Preheat the oven to 375°F (190°C). Spread the lentil mixture in the bottom of a baking dish. Top with the mashed potatoes, spreading them evenly over the filling. Use a fork to create a decorative pattern on top.
4. Bake: Bake for 20-25 minutes, or until the top is golden and crispy. Garnish with fresh parsley and serve.

---

14. Mushroom Stroganoff with Vegan Cream

Introduction: Mushroom Stroganoff is a rich and creamy dish traditionally made with beef, but in this plant-based version, we've used mushrooms to create a hearty, umami-packed base. The vegan sour cream and cashew cream make the sauce smooth and indulgent, perfect for serving over pasta or rice.

Ingredients:

- 1 tablespoon olive oil
- 1 onion, chopped
- 2 cloves garlic, minced
- 2 cups cremini or button mushrooms, sliced
- 1 teaspoon smoked paprika
- 1/2 teaspoon thyme
- 1 cup vegetable broth
- 1/2 cup white citrus (optional)
- 1/2 cup vegan sour cream
- 1/4 cup cashew cream (or coconut cream)
- Salt and pepper, to taste
- Fresh parsley, chopped, for garnish
- Cooked pasta or rice, for serving

Method:

1. Sauté the Mushrooms: Heat olive oil in a large skillet over medium heat. Add the onion and garlic and cook for 3-4 minutes. Add the mushrooms and cook for 10 minutes, until they release their moisture and begin to brown.
2. Simmer the Sauce: Stir in the paprika, thyme, vegetable broth, and white citrus (if using). Bring to a simmer and cook for 5-7 minutes, until the sauce thickens slightly.
3. Finish the Stroganoff: Lower the heat and stir in the vegan sour cream and cashew cream. Simmer for another 3-4 minutes, allowing the sauce to become creamy. Season with salt and pepper to taste.
4. Serve: Serve the mushroom stroganoff over cooked pasta or rice. Garnish with fresh parsley before serving.

---

15. Spaghetti Squash Primavera

Introduction: This Spaghetti Squash Primavera is a light and healthy dish that's perfect for spring and summer. The spaghetti squash serves as a low-carb substitute for pasta, while the colorful mix of vegetables adds freshness, crunch, and flavor. Tossed in a light garlic and olive oil dressing, this dish is simple yet satisfying.

Ingredients:

- 1 medium spaghetti squash
- 1 tablespoon olive oil
- 1 zucchini, sliced
- 1 bell pepper, sliced
- 1/2 cup cherry tomatoes, halved
- 2 cloves garlic, minced
- 1/4 cup fresh basil, chopped
- Salt and pepper, to taste
- Nutritional yeast or vegan Parmesan, for serving

Method:

1. Cook the Spaghetti Squash: Preheat the oven to 375°F (190°C). Cut the spaghetti squash in half lengthwise and scoop out the seeds. Place the squash halves on a baking sheet, cut side down. Roast for 35-40 minutes, or until the squash is tender and the strands separate easily with a fork.
2. Sauté the Vegetables: While the squash is roasting, heat olive oil in a skillet over medium heat. Add the zucchini, bell pepper, and cherry tomatoes. Cook for 5-7 minutes, until the vegetables are tender.
3. Combine the Dish: Once the squash is cooked, use a fork to scrape the flesh into spaghetti-like strands. Toss the spaghetti squash with the sautéed vegetables and minced garlic. Season with salt and pepper.

4. Serve: Garnish with fresh basil and sprinkle with nutritional yeast or vegan Parmesan. Serve immediately.

16. Roasted Brussels Sprouts with Maple Glaze

Introduction: Brussels sprouts are a versatile vegetable that can easily become the star of any meal. When roasted to perfection, they develop a delicious caramelized exterior and tender interior. The addition of a sweet maple glaze provides the perfect balance to the natural bitterness of the Brussels sprouts, making this dish a crowd-pleaser.

Ingredients:

- 1 lb Brussels sprouts, trimmed and halved
- 2 tablespoons olive oil
- Salt and pepper, to taste
- 2 tablespoons maple syrup
- 1 tablespoon balsamic vinegar
- 1 teaspoon Dijon mustard
- 1/4 teaspoon red pepper flakes (optional)
- Fresh thyme, for garnish (optional)

Method:

1. Preheat the Oven: Preheat your oven to 400°F (200°C).
2. Prepare the Brussels Sprouts: Toss the Brussels sprouts with olive oil, salt, and pepper. Arrange them in a single layer on a baking sheet, cut side down.
3. Roast: Roast for 20-25 minutes, flipping halfway through, until the Brussels sprouts are golden brown and crispy on the edges.
4. Make the Maple Glaze: In a small bowl, whisk together the maple syrup, balsamic vinegar, Dijon mustard, and red pepper flakes (if using).
5. Glaze and Serve: Once the Brussels sprouts are roasted, drizzle the maple glaze over the top and toss to coat. Garnish with fresh thyme and serve.

17. Sweet Potato and Black Bean Enchiladas

Introduction: These Sweet Potato and Black Bean Enchiladas are a perfect combination of hearty and flavorful. The sweetness of roasted sweet potatoes pairs beautifully with the savory black beans and spicy enchilada sauce, all wrapped up in soft corn tortillas. It's a comforting and satisfying meal that works well for any weeknight dinner.

Ingredients:

- 2 medium sweet potatoes, peeled and diced
- 1 tablespoon olive oil
- Salt and pepper, to taste
- 1 can (15 oz) black beans, drained and rinsed
- 1 cup frozen corn kernels
- 1 cup diced onions
- 2 teaspoons ground cumin
- 1 teaspoon chili powder
- 1/2 cup fresh cilantro, chopped
- 10 corn tortillas
- 2 cups enchilada sauce (store-bought or homemade)
- 1/2 cup vegan cheese (optional)
- Lime wedges, for serving

Method:

1. Roast the Sweet Potatoes: Preheat your oven to 400°F (200°C). Toss the diced sweet potatoes with olive oil, salt, and pepper. Roast for 20-25 minutes, or until the sweet potatoes are tender and slightly caramelized.
2. Prepare the Filling: In a large bowl, combine the roasted sweet potatoes, black beans, corn, onions, cumin, chili powder, and cilantro. Mix well to combine.
3. Assemble the Enchiladas: Preheat the oven to 375°F (190°C). Lightly oil a 9x13-inch baking dish. Warm the tortillas slightly in the microwave so they are easier to roll. Spoon a generous amount of the filling into the center of each tortilla, roll them up, and place them seam side down in the prepared baking dish.
4. Top and Bake: Pour the enchilada sauce over the rolled tortillas, then sprinkle with vegan cheese, if using. Cover with foil and bake for 25-30 minutes. Remove the foil and bake for an additional 5 minutes to brown the cheese.
5. Serve: Serve the enchiladas with lime wedges and extra fresh cilantro.

18. Spinach and Feta Stuffed Portobellos

Introduction: Spinach and Feta Stuffed Portobello Mushrooms are a fantastic way to enjoy hearty, meaty mushrooms in a vegetarian dish. The mushrooms are stuffed with a savory mixture of spinach, feta, and garlic, creating a rich, flavorful filling that's perfect for a light lunch or dinner.

Ingredients:

- 4 large Portobello mushrooms, stems removed and gills scraped
- 1 tablespoon olive oil

- 2 cups fresh spinach, chopped
- 1/2 cup crumbled feta cheese
- 2 cloves garlic, minced
- 1 tablespoon lemon juice
- 1/4 teaspoon dried oregano
- Salt and pepper, to taste
- 1/4 cup breadcrumbs (optional)
- Fresh parsley, chopped, for garnish

Method:

1. Prepare the Mushrooms: Preheat the oven to 375°F (190°C). Brush both sides of the mushrooms with olive oil and place them on a baking sheet, gill side up.
2. Make the Filling: In a pan, heat a tablespoon of olive oil over medium heat. Add the spinach and cook until wilted, about 2-3 minutes. Remove from heat and stir in the feta cheese, garlic, lemon juice, oregano, salt, and pepper.
3. Stuff the Mushrooms: Spoon the spinach and feta mixture into the mushroom caps, packing it in gently. If desired, sprinkle the tops with breadcrumbs for extra texture.
4. Bake: Bake for 15-20 minutes, or until the mushrooms are tender and the filling is golden brown.
5. Serve: Garnish with fresh parsley and serve immediately.

---

19. Vegan Chili with Avocado and Lime

Introduction: This Vegan Chili is hearty, spicy, and full of flavor. Packed with kidney beans, black beans, and vegetables, it's the perfect comfort food for cooler weather. The addition of creamy avocado and a squeeze of fresh lime provides a refreshing contrast to the warmth and spice of the chili.

Ingredients:

- 1 tablespoon olive oil
- 1 onion, chopped
- 2 cloves garlic, minced
- 1 red bell pepper, chopped
- 1 green bell pepper, chopped
- 2 carrots, diced
- 1 zucchini, diced
- 1 can (15 oz) kidney beans, drained and rinsed
- 1 can (15 oz) black beans, drained and rinsed
- 1 can (14 oz) diced tomatoes

- 1 cup vegetable broth
- 2 tablespoons chili powder
- 1 teaspoon cumin
- 1 teaspoon smoked paprika
- 1/4 teaspoon cayenne pepper (optional)
- Salt and pepper, to taste
- 1 avocado, diced
- Fresh lime wedges, for serving
- Fresh cilantro, for garnish

Method:

1. Sauté the Vegetables: Heat olive oil in a large pot over medium heat. Add the onion and garlic and sauté for 3-4 minutes until softened. Add the bell peppers, carrots, and zucchini and cook for another 5 minutes.
2. Simmer the Chili: Stir in the kidney beans, black beans, diced tomatoes, vegetable broth, chili powder, cumin, smoked paprika, cayenne (if using), salt, and pepper. Bring to a simmer and cook for 25-30 minutes, allowing the flavors to meld together.
3. Serve: Ladle the chili into bowls and top with diced avocado, fresh lime juice, and a sprinkle of cilantro.

---

20. Cauliflower Fried Rice with Ginger

Introduction: A healthy and flavorful alternative to traditional fried rice, Cauliflower Fried Rice is a low-carb dish that's packed with vegetables and a savory mix of ginger and soy sauce. It's a great way to use cauliflower as a rice substitute while still enjoying a deliciously satisfying meal.

Ingredients:

- 1 medium head of cauliflower, grated or processed into rice-sized pieces
- 2 tablespoons sesame oil
- 1 onion, chopped
- 2 cloves garlic, minced
- 1 cup mixed vegetables (e.g., peas, carrots, corn)
- 2 tablespoons soy sauce or tamari (for gluten-free)
- 1 tablespoon rice vinegar
- 1 teaspoon fresh ginger, grated
- 2 green onions, chopped
- 2 tablespoons toasted sesame seeds (optional)

Method:

1. Prepare the Cauliflower Rice: Grate the cauliflower using a box grater or pulse it in a food processor until it resembles rice grains.
2. Cook the Vegetables: Heat sesame oil in a large skillet or wok over medium heat. Add the onion and garlic and sauté for 3-4 minutes until fragrant. Add the mixed vegetables and cook for 3-5 minutes until tender.
3. Fry the Cauliflower Rice: Stir in the cauliflower rice, soy sauce, rice vinegar, and ginger. Cook, stirring occasionally, for 5-7 minutes, until the cauliflower is tender and slightly golden.
4. Serve: Top with chopped green onions and sesame seeds before serving.

Conclusion of the Chapter

The Vegetarian and Plant-Based Dishes chapter has introduced you to a diverse range of plant-forward recipes that highlight the best in seasonal ingredients, spices, and textures. From comforting soups to vibrant salads and hearty mains, these dishes show how plant-based cooking can be both delicious and satisfying. Whether you're a dedicated vegetarian or simply looking to incorporate more plant-based meals into your routine, these recipes provide a beautiful array of options to enjoy.

Chapter 8: Pasta and Grains – Elevating Everyday Ingredients

In this chapter, we explore the versatile world of pasta and grains, two essential staples that form the backbone of so many beloved dishes. Whether you're making an elegant seafood linguine or a comforting bowl of creamy risotto, pasta and grains are ingredients that offer endless possibilities. They can be elevated with a few simple ingredients and techniques, turning even the most basic dish into a masterpiece. From rich and indulgent to fresh and vibrant, these recipes celebrate both classic and contemporary takes on pasta and grain-based dishes.

1. Black Pepper and Parmesan Cacio e Pepe

Introduction:
Cacio e Pepe is a classic Roman dish that is deceptively simple, yet incredibly flavorful. The name translates to "cheese and pepper," which highlights the two key ingredients in this dish: Pecorino Romano cheese and freshly cracked black pepper. The simplicity of the ingredients makes it essential to use the best quality cheese and pepper, allowing the flavors to shine.

Ingredients:

- 12 oz spaghetti (or bucatini)
- 1 tablespoon unsalted butter
- 1 tablespoon olive oil
- 2 teaspoons freshly cracked black pepper
- 1 1/2 cups Pecorino Romano cheese, finely grated
- Salt, for pasta water
- Fresh parsley, for garnish (optional)

Method:

1. Cook the Pasta: Bring a large pot of salted water to a boil. Add the spaghetti and cook until al dente, about 8-10 minutes. Reserve 1 cup of pasta water before draining.
2. Toast the Pepper: In a large skillet, heat the olive oil and butter over medium heat. Add the cracked black pepper and toast it for about 1 minute, allowing the pepper to release its aromatic oils.

3. Combine Pasta and Sauce: Add the cooked pasta to the skillet and toss it with the pepper. Slowly add some reserved pasta water, about 1/4 cup at a time, stirring to create a creamy sauce.
4. Finish the Dish: Remove the skillet from heat and stir in the grated Pecorino Romano cheese. Continue tossing until the cheese melts and the sauce becomes creamy. Adjust with more pasta water if needed.
5. Serve: Plate the pasta and garnish with freshly chopped parsley, if desired. Serve immediately.

---

2. Lobster and Shrimp Linguine

Introduction:
A luxurious seafood dish, Lobster and Shrimp Linguine is perfect for special occasions. The sweetness of the lobster and the brininess of the shrimp are complemented by the rich, buttery sauce and the delicate strands of linguine. This dish captures the essence of the ocean and brings it right to your dinner table.

Ingredients:

- 1 lobster tail, cooked and meat removed, chopped
- 1/2 lb shrimp, peeled and deveined
- 12 oz linguine
- 1/4 cup olive oil
- 4 cloves garlic, minced
- 1/2 cup dry white citrus
- 1 cup heavy cream
- 1 tablespoon lemon zest
- 1/4 cup fresh parsley, chopped
- Salt and freshly cracked black pepper, to taste

Method:

1. Cook the Pasta: Bring a large pot of salted water to a boil. Add the linguine and cook according to package instructions until al dente. Drain and reserve some pasta water.
2. Prepare the Seafood: In a large skillet, heat olive oil over medium-high heat. Add the shrimp and cook for 2-3 minutes until pink. Remove from the skillet and set aside. In the same skillet, add the lobster meat and cook for 1-2 minutes. Remove and set aside with the shrimp.
3. Make the Sauce: In the same skillet, add garlic and cook until fragrant, about 1 minute. Add the white citrus and let it simmer until reduced by half. Add the heavy cream and simmer for 2-3 minutes until slightly thickened.

4. Combine Pasta and Seafood: Add the cooked linguine to the skillet with the sauce. Toss to coat the pasta with the sauce, adding reserved pasta water if necessary. Stir in the cooked lobster and shrimp.
5. Finish and Serve: Stir in lemon zest and fresh parsley. Season with salt and pepper to taste. Serve immediately, garnished with additional parsley.

---

3. Mushroom Risotto with Truffle Essence

Introduction:

Risotto is a dish that requires patience and a delicate touch, but the results are always worth the effort. This Mushroom Risotto with Truffle Essence is the epitome of indulgence, with earthy mushrooms and the rich, luxurious aroma of truffle oil. It's creamy, comforting, and perfect for any special occasion.

Ingredients:

- 1 1/2 cups Arborio rice
- 4 cups vegetable broth
- 2 tablespoons unsalted butter
- 1 tablespoon olive oil
- 1 small onion, finely chopped
- 2 cloves garlic, minced
- 1 lb mixed mushrooms (cremini, shiitake, portobello), sliced
- 1/2 cup dry white citrus
- 1/2 cup freshly grated Parmesan cheese
- 1 tablespoon truffle oil
- Salt and freshly cracked black pepper, to taste
- Fresh parsley, for garnish

Method:

1. Prepare the Broth: In a saucepan, keep the vegetable broth warm over low heat.
2. Sauté the Vegetables: In a large skillet, heat olive oil and butter over medium heat. Add the onions and cook until softened, about 3-4 minutes. Add the garlic and mushrooms and cook until the mushrooms are tender and release their moisture, about 5-7 minutes.
3. Cook the Rice: Add the Arborio rice to the skillet and stir to coat with the butter and oil. Cook for 1-2 minutes until the rice is lightly toasted.
4. Add the Citrus: Pour in the white citrus and stir until it's absorbed by the rice.
5. Simmer the Risotto: Begin adding the warm vegetable broth, one ladle at a time, stirring constantly and allowing each addition to be absorbed before adding more. Continue this process for about 20-25 minutes until the rice is creamy and tender.

6. Finish the Dish: Once the risotto is cooked, stir in the Parmesan cheese and truffle oil. Season with salt and pepper to taste.
7. Serve: Garnish with fresh parsley and additional Parmesan cheese, if desired. Serve immediately.

4. Creamy Pesto Penne with Grilled Zucchini

Introduction:
A rich, creamy pesto sauce paired with penne and grilled zucchini makes for a wonderfully flavorful and satisfying meal. The creamy texture of the sauce contrasts beautifully with the charred sweetness of the zucchini, creating a dish that is both comforting and fresh.

Ingredients:

- 12 oz penne pasta
- 2 medium zucchinis, sliced into rounds
- 1 tablespoon olive oil
- Salt and pepper, to taste
- 1/2 cup pesto (store-bought or homemade)
- 1/2 cup heavy cream
- 1/2 cup grated Parmesan cheese
- 1 tablespoon fresh basil, chopped

Method:

1. Cook the Pasta: Bring a large pot of salted water to a boil. Add the penne and cook until al dente, about 8-10 minutes. Drain and set aside.
2. Grill the Zucchini: Preheat a grill or grill pan over medium heat. Drizzle the zucchini slices with olive oil and season with salt and pepper. Grill for 2-3 minutes per side, until charred and tender.
3. Make the Sauce: In a saucepan, combine the pesto, heavy cream, and Parmesan cheese. Cook over low heat, stirring constantly, until the sauce is smooth and heated through.
4. Combine: Toss the cooked penne with the creamy pesto sauce. Add the grilled zucchini and toss gently to combine.
5. Serve: Garnish with fresh basil and serve immediately.

5. Mediterranean Couscous Salad

Introduction:
Couscous, often considered a grain, is a small, round pasta that absorbs flavors beautifully. This Mediterranean Couscous Salad is fresh, light, and bursting with vibrant ingredients like cucumber, tomatoes, and olives, dressed in a zesty lemon vinaigrette. It's perfect as a side dish or a light lunch.

Ingredients:

- 1 cup couscous
- 1 1/4 cups boiling water
- 1/2 cucumber, diced
- 1/2 cup cherry tomatoes, halved
- 1/4 cup Kalamata olives, pitted and chopped
- 1/4 cup red onion, finely diced
- 2 tablespoons fresh parsley, chopped
- 2 tablespoons olive oil
- Juice of 1 lemon
- 1 teaspoon red citrus vinegar
- Salt and freshly cracked black pepper, to taste

Method:

1. Prepare the Couscous: In a large bowl, pour the boiling water over the couscous. Cover with a lid or plastic wrap and let it steam for 5 minutes. Fluff with a fork to separate the grains.
2. Make the Dressing: In a small bowl, whisk together the olive oil, lemon juice, red citrus vinegar, salt, and pepper.
3. Assemble the Salad: In a large bowl, combine the couscous, cucumber, tomatoes, olives, onion, and parsley. Drizzle with the dressing and toss to combine.
4. Serve: Serve immediately or chill in the fridge for 30 minutes before serving.

6. Wild Mushroom and Asparagus Farro

Introduction:
Farro, an ancient grain with a nutty flavor and chewy texture, is a perfect base for hearty, savory dishes like this Wild Mushroom and Asparagus Farro. The combination of earthy mushrooms, tender asparagus, and the distinct flavor of farro is complemented by a touch of garlic and Parmesan. This dish is as filling as it is healthy, making it a great choice for a meatless meal or as a side to accompany a protein.

Ingredients:

- 1 cup farro
- 3 cups vegetable broth
- 1 tablespoon olive oil
- 1/2 onion, diced
- 3 cloves garlic, minced
- 1 lb mixed wild mushrooms (shiitake, cremini, chanterelles), sliced
- 1 bunch asparagus, trimmed and cut into 1-inch pieces
- 1/4 cup white citrus
- 1/4 cup grated Parmesan cheese
- Salt and freshly cracked black pepper, to taste
- Fresh thyme, for garnish

Method:

1. Cook the Farro: In a medium saucepan, bring the vegetable broth to a boil. Add the farro, reduce the heat, and simmer for 20-25 minutes until tender. Drain any excess liquid and set aside.
2. Sauté the Vegetables: In a large skillet, heat olive oil over medium heat. Add the onion and garlic and sauté for 3-4 minutes until softened. Add the mushrooms and cook for another 5-7 minutes until they release their moisture and become golden brown.
3. Add the Asparagus: Add the asparagus to the skillet and cook for an additional 3-4 minutes, until tender but still crisp.
4. Deglaze the Pan: Pour in the white citrus and cook for 2-3 minutes, allowing the liquid to reduce.
5. Combine: Add the cooked farro to the skillet and toss to combine with the vegetables. Stir in the Parmesan cheese and season with salt and pepper to taste.
6. Serve: Garnish with fresh thyme and serve immediately.

---

7. Seafood Paella with Saffron

Introduction:

Paella is one of Spain's most iconic dishes, traditionally made with a variety of seafood, chicken, and rice. This Seafood Paella with Saffron is a celebration of the ocean, infused with the rich flavors of saffron and paprika. The long, slow cooking process allows the rice to absorb all the savory juices from the seafood, creating a dish that's both luxurious and comforting.

Ingredients:

- 1 1/2 cups short-grain Spanish rice (like Bomba or Arborio)
- 3 tablespoons olive oil

- 1 onion, finely chopped
- 1 bell pepper, diced
- 4 cloves garlic, minced
- 1/2 teaspoon smoked paprika
- 1/2 teaspoon saffron threads, soaked in 2 tablespoons warm water
- 1 1/2 cups chicken broth
- 1 cup dry white citrus
- 1 lb shrimp, peeled and deveined
- 1/2 lb mussels, cleaned
- 1/2 lb squid, sliced into rings
- 1/2 lb clams, cleaned
- 1/2 cup frozen peas
- Salt and freshly cracked black pepper, to taste
- Lemon wedges, for garnish
- Fresh parsley, chopped, for garnish

Method:

1. Prepare the Rice: In a large paella pan or wide skillet, heat olive oil over medium heat. Add the onion and bell pepper, and cook until softened, about 5 minutes.
2. Add Garlic and Spices: Stir in the garlic, smoked paprika, and saffron with its soaking liquid. Cook for 1-2 minutes until fragrant.
3. Cook the Rice: Add the rice to the pan, stirring to coat it with the spices and vegetables. Pour in the chicken broth and white citrus. Bring to a simmer and cook for 15-20 minutes, without stirring, until the rice has absorbed most of the liquid.
4. Add the Seafood: Arrange the shrimp, mussels, squid, and clams on top of the rice. Cover the pan with a lid or aluminum foil and cook for an additional 5-7 minutes until the seafood is cooked through and the rice is tender.
5. Finish the Dish: Stir in the frozen peas and cook for 2 more minutes.
6. Serve: Garnish with fresh parsley and lemon wedges. Serve immediately.

8. Spaghetti Carbonara with Pancetta

Introduction:
The beauty of Spaghetti Carbonara lies in its simplicity. This classic Italian dish combines the richness of egg, cheese, and pancetta in a creamy sauce that coats the pasta perfectly. The key to a perfect Carbonara is the balance of flavors and textures, with crispy pancetta and a smooth, velvety sauce that doesn't curdle.

Ingredients:

- 12 oz spaghetti
- 4 oz pancetta, diced
- 2 large eggs
- 1 cup grated Pecorino Romano cheese
- 1/2 cup grated Parmesan cheese
- Freshly cracked black pepper, to taste
- Salt, for pasta water
- Fresh parsley, for garnish

Method:

1. Cook the Pasta: Bring a large pot of salted water to a boil. Add the spaghetti and cook until al dente, about 8-10 minutes. Reserve 1/2 cup of pasta water before draining.
2. Cook the Pancetta: While the pasta cooks, heat a large skillet over medium heat. Add the diced pancetta and cook until crispy, about 5 minutes. Remove from the heat and set aside.
3. Prepare the Sauce: In a bowl, whisk together the eggs, Pecorino Romano, Parmesan, and a generous amount of black pepper.
4. Combine the Pasta and Sauce: Add the drained pasta to the skillet with the pancetta and toss to combine. Slowly add the egg mixture, tossing quickly to create a creamy sauce. Add reserved pasta water a little at a time to adjust the consistency of the sauce.
5. Serve: Serve immediately, garnished with extra cheese and parsley.

9. Butternut Squash Risotto

Introduction:

This creamy Butternut Squash Risotto is a perfect fall dish that showcases the natural sweetness of the squash, which pairs beautifully with the rich, creamy texture of the risotto. The addition of sage and Parmesan adds a layer of warmth and depth to the dish.

Ingredients:

- 1 cup Arborio rice
- 3 cups chicken or vegetable broth
- 1 tablespoon olive oil
- 1/2 onion, diced
- 2 cloves garlic, minced
- 1 small butternut squash, peeled and diced
- 1/4 cup dry white citrus

- 1/4 cup heavy cream
- 1/4 cup grated Parmesan cheese
- 1/4 teaspoon ground sage
- Salt and freshly cracked black pepper, to taste

Method:

1. Roast the Squash: Preheat the oven to 400°F (200°C). Spread the diced butternut squash on a baking sheet and drizzle with olive oil. Season with salt and pepper. Roast for 25-30 minutes until tender and caramelized.
2. Cook the Risotto: In a saucepan, bring the broth to a simmer. In a separate large pan, heat olive oil over medium heat. Add the onion and garlic, and sauté for 3-4 minutes until softened. Add the Arborio rice and toast for 1-2 minutes.
3. Deglaze and Simmer: Pour in the white citrus and cook until it's absorbed. Begin adding the warm broth, one ladleful at a time, stirring constantly and allowing the liquid to be absorbed before adding more. Continue until the rice is tender and creamy, about 18-20 minutes.
4. Finish the Risotto: Stir in the roasted butternut squash, heavy cream, Parmesan cheese, and sage. Season with salt and pepper to taste.
5. Serve: Serve the risotto immediately, garnished with extra Parmesan cheese if desired.

---

10. Spinach and Ricotta Stuffed Shells

Introduction:
Spinach and Ricotta Stuffed Shells are the epitome of comfort food. Jumbo pasta shells are filled with a creamy mixture of ricotta cheese, spinach, and herbs, then baked in a rich marinara sauce until bubbling and golden. This dish is perfect for a family dinner or for making ahead and reheating.

Ingredients:

- 12 jumbo pasta shells
- 2 cups ricotta cheese
- 1 cup cooked spinach, squeezed dry and chopped
- 1 egg
- 1/2 cup grated Parmesan cheese
- 2 cups marinara sauce
- 1/2 teaspoon dried oregano
- Salt and freshly cracked black pepper, to taste
- Fresh basil, for garnish

Method:

1. Cook the Shells: Preheat the oven to 375°F (190°C). Cook the pasta shells in a large pot of salted water according to package instructions until al dente. Drain and set aside to cool.
2. Prepare the Filling: In a bowl, mix the ricotta cheese, cooked spinach, egg, Parmesan cheese, oregano, salt, and pepper.
3. Stuff the Shells: Fill each cooked shell with the ricotta and spinach mixture and place them in a baking dish. Pour marinara sauce over the shells, covering them completely.
4. Bake: Cover the dish with foil and bake for 25 minutes. Remove the foil and bake for an additional 10 minutes, until the top is golden and bubbly.
5. Serve: Garnish with fresh basil and serve.

11. Shrimp Jambalaya

Introduction:

Jambalaya is a beloved Southern dish that brings together a medley of flavors from the Cajun and Creole culinary traditions. This Shrimp Jambalaya features succulent shrimp, rice, vegetables, and a hint of spice, all simmered together to create a flavorful and hearty meal. It's a one-pot wonder that's perfect for family dinners or gatherings.

Ingredients:

*   1 lb large shrimp, peeled and deveined
*   2 tablespoons olive oil
*   1 onion, diced
*   1 bell pepper, diced
*   2 stalks celery, diced
*   3 cloves garlic, minced
*   1 can (14 oz) diced tomatoes
*   1 cup long-grain white rice
*   2 cups chicken broth
*   1 teaspoon smoked paprika
*   1 teaspoon dried thyme
*   1/2 teaspoon cayenne pepper
*   Salt and freshly cracked black pepper, to taste
*   1/4 cup chopped fresh parsley, for garnish
*   Lemon wedges, for serving

Method:

1. Sauté the Vegetables: In a large pot or Dutch oven, heat the olive oil over medium heat. Add the onion, bell pepper, and celery, and cook for 5-7 minutes until softened. Stir in the garlic and cook for an additional 1 minute.
2. Add the Rice and Spices: Stir in the rice, smoked paprika, thyme, cayenne pepper, salt, and pepper. Cook for 2-3 minutes to toast the rice slightly.
3. Simmer the Jambalaya: Add the diced tomatoes and chicken broth, stirring to combine. Bring the mixture to a boil, then reduce the heat, cover, and simmer for 20-25 minutes, until the rice is tender and the liquid is absorbed.
4. Cook the Shrimp: While the rice is cooking, season the shrimp with salt and pepper. In a separate pan, sauté the shrimp in a little olive oil for 2-3 minutes on each side, until pink and cooked through.
5. Combine and Serve: Once the rice is cooked, gently fold in the shrimp. Garnish with fresh parsley and serve with lemon wedges.

12. Greek Orzo Salad

Introduction:
This Greek Orzo Salad is a vibrant, fresh, and healthy side dish that brings together the bright flavors of the Mediterranean. The orzo pasta is tossed with tomatoes, cucumbers, Kalamata olives, feta cheese, and a tangy lemon-oregano vinaigrette, making it the perfect addition to any meal.

Ingredients:

- 1 lb orzo pasta
- 1 cucumber, diced
- 1 pint cherry tomatoes, halved
- 1/2 red onion, thinly sliced
- 1/2 cup Kalamata olives, pitted and sliced
- 1/2 cup crumbled feta cheese
- 1/4 cup extra virgin olive oil
- 2 tablespoons red citrus vinegar
- 1 teaspoon dried oregano
- 1 lemon, juiced
- Salt and freshly cracked black pepper, to taste

Method:

1. Cook the Orzo: Cook the orzo according to package instructions. Drain and rinse under cold water to cool it down. Transfer to a large bowl.
2. Prepare the Salad: Add the cucumber, cherry tomatoes, red onion, olives, and feta to the cooled orzo.

3. Make the Dressing: In a small bowl, whisk together the olive oil, red citrus vinegar, oregano, lemon juice, salt, and pepper.
4. Toss the Salad: Pour the dressing over the salad and toss to combine. Adjust seasoning as needed.
5. Serve: Chill the salad in the refrigerator for 30 minutes before serving for the flavors to meld together.

---

13. Gnocchi with Brown Butter and Sage

Introduction:
Gnocchi with Brown Butter and Sage is a rich and comforting Italian dish that highlights the delicate texture of potato gnocchi. The nutty brown butter, combined with the fragrant sage, creates a simple yet luxurious sauce that beautifully coats the gnocchi.

Ingredients:

- 1 lb potato gnocchi (store-bought or homemade)
- 4 tablespoons unsalted butter
- 12-15 fresh sage leaves
- 1/4 cup grated Parmesan cheese
- Salt and freshly cracked black pepper, to taste

Method:

1. Cook the Gnocchi: Bring a large pot of salted water to a boil. Add the gnocchi and cook until they float to the surface, about 2-3 minutes. Remove with a slotted spoon and set aside.
2. Brown the Butter: In a large skillet, melt the butter over medium heat. Add the sage leaves and cook for 2-3 minutes, swirling the pan occasionally, until the butter becomes golden brown and fragrant.
3. Toss the Gnocchi: Add the cooked gnocchi to the skillet and toss gently to coat in the brown butter and sage sauce. Season with salt and pepper to taste.
4. Serve: Sprinkle with grated Parmesan cheese and serve immediately.

---

14. Lemon and Herb Quinoa Pilaf

Introduction:
This Lemon and Herb Quinoa Pilaf is a light, fragrant, and protein-packed side dish that pairs beautifully with any meal. The quinoa is cooked with a combination of fresh herbs

and lemon, which imparts a fresh and zesty flavor, making it a perfect complement to grilled meats, seafood, or roasted vegetables.

Ingredients:

- 1 cup quinoa
- 2 cups vegetable broth or water
- 1 tablespoon olive oil
- 1/2 small onion, diced
- 2 cloves garlic, minced
- 1/4 cup chopped fresh parsley
- 1/4 cup chopped fresh cilantro
- Zest of 1 lemon
- Juice of 1 lemon
- Salt and freshly cracked black pepper, to taste

Method:

1. Cook the Quinoa: In a medium saucepan, bring the vegetable broth or water to a boil. Add the quinoa, reduce the heat to low, cover, and simmer for 15-18 minutes, until the quinoa is tender and the liquid is absorbed. Fluff with a fork and set aside.
2. Sauté the Aromatics: In a skillet, heat olive oil over medium heat. Add the onion and garlic, and cook for 3-4 minutes until softened.
3. Combine the Quinoa: Stir in the cooked quinoa, parsley, cilantro, lemon zest, and lemon juice. Season with salt and pepper to taste.
4. Serve: Serve warm as a side dish.

---

15. Pasta Bolognese with Fresh Herbs

Introduction:
Pasta Bolognese is a rich and savory Italian classic, featuring a slow-cooked meat sauce that's perfect for pairing with pasta. This version uses fresh herbs like basil and thyme to enhance the depth of flavor, creating a hearty dish that's both satisfying and comforting.

Ingredients:

- 1 lb ground beef or beef
- 1/2 onion, diced
- 2 cloves garlic, minced
- 1 can (14 oz) crushed tomatoes
- 1/2 cup red citrus
- 1 tablespoon tomato paste

- 1/2 cup whole milk or cream
- 1 teaspoon dried thyme
- 1 teaspoon dried oregano
- 1/4 cup fresh basil, chopped
- Salt and freshly cracked black pepper, to taste
- 12 oz pasta (pappardelle, fettuccine, or tagliatelle)
- Freshly grated Parmesan cheese, for serving

Method:

1. Cook the Meat: In a large skillet, brown the ground beef or beef over medium heat until fully cooked, about 8-10 minutes. Remove any excess fat.
2. Add the Aromatics: Add the diced onion and minced garlic to the skillet and cook for 3-4 minutes, until softened.
3. Simmer the Sauce: Stir in the crushed tomatoes, red citrus, tomato paste, thyme, and oregano. Bring to a simmer and cook for 25-30 minutes, allowing the flavors to develop and the sauce to thicken. Add the milk or cream and stir to combine.
4. Cook the Pasta: While the sauce simmers, cook the pasta in a large pot of salted water according to package instructions. Drain and set aside.
5. Serve: Toss the cooked pasta with the Bolognese sauce. Garnish with fresh basil and grated Parmesan cheese before serving.

16. Vegetable Biryani

Introduction:

Vegetable Biryani is a fragrant and flavorful rice dish that's commonly enjoyed in Indian cuisine. It's made with basmati rice, a variety of colorful vegetables, and a blend of aromatic spices like cumin, coriander, and cardamom. This dish can be served as a main course or as a side dish with yogurt or raita.

Ingredients:

- 1 1/2 cups basmati rice
- 2 tablespoons vegetable oil
- 1 onion, thinly sliced
- 1 carrot, julienned
- 1 bell pepper, diced
- 1 cup frozen peas
- 2 cloves garlic, minced
- 1 tablespoon ginger, grated
- 1/2 teaspoon cumin seeds

- 1/2 teaspoon ground coriander
- 1/4 teaspoon ground turmeric
- 1 cinnamon stick
- 3-4 cardamom pods
- 1 bay leaf
- 3 cups vegetable broth
- Salt and freshly cracked black pepper, to taste
- Fresh cilantro, for garnish
- Yogurt, for serving (optional)

Method:

1. Cook the Rice: Rinse the basmati rice under cold water until the water runs clear. In a large pot, bring 3 cups of vegetable broth to a boil. Add the rice, and cook until tender, about 12-15 minutes. Drain and set aside.
2. Prepare the Vegetables: In a large skillet, heat the oil over medium heat. Add the onion and cook for 5-7 minutes, until golden brown. Add the garlic, ginger, and spices, and cook for another minute until fragrant.
3. Combine the Vegetables: Add the carrot, bell pepper, and peas to the skillet, cooking for 3-4 minutes. Stir in the cooked rice, season with salt and pepper, and mix well.
4. Serve: Garnish with fresh cilantro and serve with yogurt on the side, if desired.

---

17. Classic Macaroni and Cheese

Introduction:
There's nothing more comforting than a warm bowl of Classic Macaroni and Cheese. This rich, creamy dish combines tender elbow macaroni with a velvety cheese sauce, topped with breadcrumbs for a little crunch. It's a perfect family meal, and the ultimate comfort food.

Ingredients:

- 1 lb elbow macaroni
- 4 tablespoons unsalted butter
- 1/4 cup all-purpose flour
- 4 cups whole milk
- 2 cups shredded sharp cheddar cheese
- 1 cup shredded Gruyère cheese
- 1/2 teaspoon mustard powder
- 1/4 teaspoon cayenne pepper
- Salt and freshly cracked black pepper, to taste

- 1/2 cup panko breadcrumbs

Method:

1. Cook the Macaroni: Bring a large pot of salted water to a boil. Cook the elbow macaroni according to package instructions. Drain and set aside.
2. Make the Cheese Sauce: In a saucepan, melt the butter over medium heat. Whisk in the flour and cook for 1-2 minutes, until golden. Slowly add the milk, whisking constantly to avoid lumps. Bring the mixture to a simmer, and cook until it thickens, about 5 minutes.
3. Add the Cheese: Stir in the shredded cheddar and Gruyère cheeses until melted and smooth. Season with mustard powder, cayenne, salt, and pepper.
4. Combine: Toss the cooked macaroni with the cheese sauce until well coated.
5. Bake (optional): Preheat the oven to 350°F (175°C). Pour the macaroni and cheese into a baking dish. Sprinkle panko breadcrumbs on top and bake for 20 minutes, until golden and bubbly.
6. Serve: Serve warm.

18. Chicken Alfredo Fettuccine

Introduction:

Chicken Alfredo Fettuccine is a creamy, decadent pasta dish that's perfect for a comforting weeknight dinner. The rich Alfredo sauce, made with butter, cream, and Parmesan, coats the fettuccine and is complemented by tender pieces of grilled chicken.

Ingredients:

- 1 lb fettuccine pasta
- 2 chicken breasts, boneless and skinless
- 2 tablespoons olive oil
- Salt and freshly cracked black pepper, to taste
- 4 tablespoons unsalted butter
- 1 cup heavy cream
- 1 1/2 cups grated Parmesan cheese
- 1/2 teaspoon garlic powder
- Fresh parsley, for garnish

Method:

1. Cook the Pasta: Cook the fettuccine in a large pot of salted water according to package instructions. Drain and set aside.

2. Cook the Chicken: Heat olive oil in a skillet over medium heat. Season the chicken breasts with salt and pepper, and cook for 6-7 minutes per side until golden brown and cooked through. Slice the chicken into strips.
3. Make the Alfredo Sauce: In the same skillet, melt the butter over medium heat. Stir in the cream and garlic powder, bringing the mixture to a simmer. Cook for 3-4 minutes until thickened.
4. Combine: Stir in the grated Parmesan cheese until melted and smooth. Add the cooked pasta and toss to combine.
5. Serve: Top with sliced chicken and garnish with fresh parsley before serving.

19. Tomato Basil Bucatini

Introduction:
Tomato Basil Bucatini is a simple yet flavorful Italian pasta dish that highlights the natural sweetness of tomatoes and the aromatic fragrance of fresh basil. The bucatini pasta, with its hollow center, soaks up the sauce, making each bite a burst of flavor.

Ingredients:

- 1 lb bucatini pasta
- 2 tablespoons olive oil
- 2 cloves garlic, minced
- 2 cans (14 oz each) crushed tomatoes
- 1/4 cup fresh basil, chopped
- Salt and freshly cracked black pepper, to taste
- Grated Parmesan cheese, for serving

Method:

1. Cook the Pasta: Bring a large pot of salted water to a boil. Cook the bucatini according to package instructions. Drain and set aside.
2. Prepare the Sauce: Heat olive oil in a skillet over medium heat. Add the garlic and cook for 1 minute until fragrant. Stir in the crushed tomatoes, salt, and pepper. Simmer for 10 minutes to allow the flavors to meld.
3. Combine: Toss the cooked bucatini in the tomato sauce, and add the fresh basil.
4. Serve: Garnish with grated Parmesan cheese and serve.

20. Spaghetti Aglio e Olio

Introduction:
Spaghetti Aglio e Olio is one of the simplest and most flavorful Italian pasta dishes. Made with just garlic, olive oil, red pepper flakes, and parsley, this dish is a celebration of how a few basic ingredients can create a delicious, satisfying meal.

Ingredients:

- 1 lb spaghetti
- 1/4 cup extra virgin olive oil
- 5 cloves garlic, thinly sliced
- 1/2 teaspoon red pepper flakes
- Salt, to taste
- Fresh parsley, chopped, for garnish
- Grated Parmesan cheese, for serving (optional)

Method:

1. Cook the Spaghetti: Bring a large pot of salted water to a boil. Cook the spaghetti according to package instructions. Drain, reserving a cup of pasta water.
2. Prepare the Sauce: In a large skillet, heat olive oil over medium heat. Add the garlic and cook until golden brown, about 2 minutes. Add the red pepper flakes and cook for an additional 30 seconds.
3. Combine: Add the cooked spaghetti to the skillet and toss to coat in the garlic and oil. Add a splash of pasta water to help combine.
4. Serve: Garnish with fresh parsley and serve with grated Parmesan, if desired.

This concludes the Pasta and Grains chapter! Each of these recipes elevates everyday ingredients to create mouthwatering dishes. Whether you crave a rich pasta or a refreshing grain salad, these recipes offer something for every palate, with vibrant flavors and delightful textures. Enjoy!

9. Sides That Steal the Show (15 Recipes)

Introduction

Sides are often thought of as mere accompaniments to the main dish, but they can truly shine on their own. When done right, a side dish can elevate a meal and offer a refreshing contrast or complementary flavor to the main course. This chapter features 15 side dishes that go above and beyond, using bold flavors, unexpected combinations, and innovative cooking techniques to create unforgettable sides that steal the show.

1. Truffle Mac and Cheese

Introduction: Mac and cheese is a classic comfort food, but when paired with the indulgent flavors of truffle oil and creamy cheese, it becomes an irresistible side dish. This Truffle Mac and Cheese combines a velvety béchamel sauce, earthy truffle oil, and a mix of rich cheeses to create a luxurious twist on the classic.

Ingredients:

- 1 lb elbow macaroni
- 4 tablespoons unsalted butter
- 1/4 cup all-purpose flour
- 2 cups whole milk
- 1 cup heavy cream
- 2 cups grated Gruyère cheese
- 1 1/2 cups grated sharp cheddar cheese
- 1 tablespoon truffle oil (or to taste)
- Salt and freshly cracked black pepper, to taste
- 1/2 cup panko breadcrumbs
- Fresh chives, chopped (for garnish)

Method:

1. Cook the Pasta: Bring a large pot of salted water to a boil and cook the elbow macaroni according to the package instructions. Drain and set aside.
2. Make the Cheese Sauce: In a large saucepan, melt the butter over medium heat. Add the flour and cook, whisking constantly, for about 2 minutes. Gradually whisk in the milk and cream, and cook until the sauce thickens (about 5 minutes).

3. Add the Cheese: Stir in the Gruyère and cheddar cheese, allowing them to melt into the sauce. Season with salt, pepper, and truffle oil.
4. Combine and Bake (optional): Toss the cooked macaroni with the cheese sauce. Pour into a baking dish, top with panko breadcrumbs, and bake at 350°F for 15-20 minutes until the top is golden brown.
5. Serve: Garnish with fresh chives and serve.

2. Roasted Brussels Sprouts with Balsamic Glaze

Introduction: Brussels sprouts, when roasted to crispy perfection, become a caramelized treat full of rich, earthy flavors. The addition of a balsamic glaze gives this side a tangy-sweet finish that pairs beautifully with roasted meats or hearty pastas.

Ingredients:

- 1 lb Brussels sprouts, trimmed and halved
- 2 tablespoons olive oil
- Salt and freshly cracked black pepper, to taste
- 1/4 cup balsamic vinegar
- 1 tablespoon honey
- 1 tablespoon Dijon mustard (optional)

Method:

1. Roast the Brussels Sprouts: Preheat your oven to 400°F. Toss the halved Brussels sprouts with olive oil, salt, and pepper. Spread them in a single layer on a baking sheet and roast for 20-25 minutes, flipping halfway through, until crispy and golden.
2. Prepare the Balsamic Glaze: While the Brussels sprouts roast, combine the balsamic vinegar, honey, and mustard (if using) in a small saucepan. Bring to a simmer over medium heat and cook for 5-7 minutes, until thickened and syrupy.
3. Toss and Serve: Once the Brussels sprouts are roasted, drizzle the balsamic glaze over them and toss to coat. Serve immediately.

3. Garlic-Parmesan Roasted Potatoes

Introduction: Crispy on the outside and tender on the inside, these Garlic-Parmesan Roasted Potatoes are seasoned with garlic, fresh herbs, and Parmesan cheese, making them the perfect side for any meal, from grilled meats to pasta dishes.

Ingredients:

- 1 1/2 lbs baby potatoes, halved
- 3 tablespoons olive oil
- 4 cloves garlic, minced
- 1 teaspoon dried thyme
- 1 teaspoon dried rosemary
- 1/2 cup grated Parmesan cheese
- Salt and freshly cracked black pepper, to taste
- Fresh parsley, chopped (for garnish)

Method:

1. Prepare the Potatoes: Preheat your oven to 425°F. Toss the halved baby potatoes with olive oil, garlic, thyme, rosemary, salt, and pepper.
2. Roast the Potatoes: Spread the seasoned potatoes on a baking sheet in a single layer. Roast for 25-30 minutes, flipping halfway through, until golden brown and crispy.
3. Add the Parmesan: Remove the potatoes from the oven and immediately sprinkle with grated Parmesan cheese. Toss to coat.
4. Serve: Garnish with fresh parsley and serve.

---

4. Creamed Spinach with Nutmeg

Introduction: This creamy, rich side dish is a classic favorite. The creaminess of the sauce is perfectly balanced by the earthy flavor of spinach and a hint of nutmeg, making it a perfect accompaniment to steaks, roasted chicken, or holiday meals.

Ingredients:

- 2 lbs fresh spinach, washed and chopped
- 4 tablespoons unsalted butter
- 2 cloves garlic, minced
- 1 cup heavy cream
- 1/2 teaspoon freshly grated nutmeg
- Salt and freshly cracked black pepper, to taste
- 1/4 cup grated Parmesan cheese (optional)

Method:

1. Sauté the Garlic: In a large skillet, melt the butter over medium heat. Add the garlic and cook for 1-2 minutes until fragrant.

2. Wilt the Spinach: Add the spinach in batches, stirring frequently until it wilts down. Once all the spinach is in the pan, cook for an additional 3-4 minutes to release excess moisture.
3. Make the Cream Sauce: Pour in the heavy cream and season with nutmeg, salt, and pepper. Stir to combine and let the mixture simmer for 5-7 minutes until thickened.
4. Finish and Serve: Stir in Parmesan cheese, if using, and serve immediately.

---

5. Sweet Potato Fries with Garlic and Herbs

Introduction: These crispy Sweet Potato Fries are a healthier alternative to regular fries, with a naturally sweet flavor that pairs beautifully with garlic and fresh herbs. They're perfect for pairing with burgers, grilled meats, or even as a snack.

Ingredients:

- 2 large sweet potatoes, peeled and cut into fries
- 3 tablespoons olive oil
- 3 cloves garlic, minced
- 1 teaspoon dried thyme
- 1 teaspoon dried rosemary
- Salt and freshly cracked black pepper, to taste
- Fresh parsley, chopped (for garnish)

Method:

1. Prepare the Fries: Preheat your oven to 425°F. Toss the sweet potato fries with olive oil, garlic, thyme, rosemary, salt, and pepper.
2. Roast the Fries: Spread the fries in a single layer on a baking sheet. Roast for 25-30 minutes, flipping halfway through, until crispy and golden.
3. Serve: Garnish with fresh parsley and serve immediately.

---

6. Charred Corn Salad with Lime and Feta

Introduction: This Charred Corn Salad is the perfect balance of smoky, tangy, and fresh flavors. The charred corn adds depth, while the lime and feta brighten the dish, making it a great accompaniment to summer BBQs or grilled meats.

Ingredients:

- 4 ears of corn, husked
- 1/4 cup olive oil
- 1/2 red onion, finely diced
- 1 red bell pepper, diced
- 1/4 cup fresh cilantro, chopped
- 1/4 cup crumbled feta cheese
- Juice of 1 lime
- Salt and freshly cracked black pepper, to taste

Method:

1. Char the Corn: Heat a grill or grill pan over medium-high heat. Grill the corn, turning occasionally, until charred and golden on all sides (about 8-10 minutes).
2. Prepare the Salad: Once the corn has cooled slightly, cut the kernels off the cob and transfer them to a large bowl. Add the red onion, bell pepper, cilantro, and feta.
3. Season and Serve: Drizzle with lime juice, season with salt and pepper, and toss to combine. Serve immediately.

---

7. Creamy Garlic Mashed Potatoes

Introduction: No meal is complete without creamy mashed potatoes. This version uses roasted garlic and heavy cream to make the potatoes extra indulgent, perfect for pairing with everything from steak to roast chicken.

Ingredients:

- 2 lbs Yukon Gold potatoes, peeled and cut into chunks
- 4 cloves garlic, peeled
- 1/2 cup heavy cream
- 1/4 cup unsalted butter
- Salt and freshly cracked black pepper, to taste
- Fresh chives, chopped (for garnish)

Method:

1. Boil the Potatoes: Place the potatoes and garlic in a large pot and cover with cold water. Bring to a boil and cook for 15-20 minutes until tender.
2. Mash the Potatoes: Drain the potatoes and garlic, then return them to the pot. Mash until smooth and creamy.
3. Add the Cream and Butter: Stir in the heavy cream, butter, salt, and pepper. Continue mashing until smooth and creamy.
4. Serve: Garnish with fresh chives and serve.

8. Grilled Asparagus with Lemon and Parmesan

Introduction: Grilled asparagus is a perfect side for any season, offering a smoky charred flavor that contrasts wonderfully with a fresh squeeze of lemon and the savory richness of Parmesan. This simple yet elegant dish can elevate any meal, from grilled meats to pasta.

Ingredients:

- 1 bunch asparagus, trimmed
- 2 tablespoons olive oil
- Salt and freshly cracked black pepper, to taste
- Zest of 1 lemon
- 1/4 cup grated Parmesan cheese
- Fresh lemon wedges (for serving)

Method:

1. Preheat the Grill: Heat a grill or grill pan to medium-high heat.
2. Prepare the Asparagus: Toss the trimmed asparagus with olive oil, salt, and pepper.
3. Grill the Asparagus: Place the asparagus on the grill and cook for 3-5 minutes, turning occasionally, until tender and lightly charred.
4. Finish and Serve: Remove the asparagus from the grill, and while still hot, sprinkle with lemon zest and Parmesan. Serve with fresh lemon wedges on the side.

---

9. Roasted Sweet Potatoes with Maple and Cinnamon

Introduction: Sweet potatoes are naturally sweet and earthy, making them the perfect vegetable to pair with maple syrup and cinnamon for a comforting, slightly caramelized side dish. These Roasted Sweet Potatoes with Maple and Cinnamon are a great addition to any autumn or winter meal and perfect for holiday gatherings.

Ingredients:

- 2 large sweet potatoes, peeled and cut into cubes
- 2 tablespoons olive oil
- 2 tablespoons maple syrup
- 1 teaspoon ground cinnamon
- Salt and freshly cracked black pepper, to taste
- Fresh thyme leaves (optional, for garnish)

Method:

1. Preheat the Oven: Preheat your oven to 400°F.
2. Prepare the Sweet Potatoes: Toss the cubed sweet potatoes with olive oil, maple syrup, cinnamon, salt, and pepper. Spread them in a single layer on a baking sheet.
3. Roast the Sweet Potatoes: Roast for 25-30 minutes, stirring halfway through, until the sweet potatoes are tender and caramelized.
4. Serve: Garnish with fresh thyme leaves (if desired) and serve immediately.

10. Cornbread with Jalapeño and Cheddar

Introduction: Cornbread is the perfect comforting side, but when you add spicy jalapeños and sharp cheddar cheese, it becomes a standout dish that can hold its own. The moist, flavorful texture of this cornbread pairs beautifully with barbecue, chili, or a hearty stew.

Ingredients:

- 1 cup cornmeal
- 1 cup all-purpose flour
- 1 tablespoon baking powder
- 1/2 teaspoon salt
- 1/4 teaspoon ground black pepper
- 1 cup buttermilk
- 2 large eggs
- 1/4 cup unsalted butter, melted
- 1 cup sharp cheddar cheese, grated
- 2 jalapeños, seeds removed and finely chopped
- 2 tablespoons honey (optional)

Method:

1. Preheat the Oven: Preheat your oven to 375°F and grease a 9x9-inch baking pan.
2. Combine the Dry Ingredients: In a medium bowl, mix together cornmeal, flour, baking powder, salt, and pepper.
3. Mix the Wet Ingredients: In a separate bowl, whisk together buttermilk, eggs, and melted butter.
4. Combine and Add Cheese and Jalapeños: Add the wet ingredients to the dry ingredients and stir until just combined. Fold in the cheddar cheese and jalapeños.
5. Bake: Pour the batter into the prepared pan and bake for 25-30 minutes, or until a toothpick inserted into the center comes out clean.
6. Serve: Drizzle with honey, if desired, and serve warm.

11. Cauliflower Rice with Cilantro and Lime

Introduction: Cauliflower rice is a fantastic low-carb, grain-free alternative to traditional rice. This Cauliflower Rice with Cilantro and Lime adds freshness and zest, making it an ideal side dish for tacos, grilled meats, or as a light side to a heavier meal.

Ingredients:

- 1 medium head of cauliflower, chopped into florets
- 2 tablespoons olive oil
- Salt and freshly cracked black pepper, to taste
- Juice and zest of 1 lime
- 1/4 cup fresh cilantro, chopped

Method:

1. Prepare the Cauliflower: Pulse the cauliflower florets in a food processor until they resemble rice grains.
2. Cook the Cauliflower Rice: Heat olive oil in a large skillet over medium heat. Add the cauliflower rice and sauté for 5-7 minutes, stirring frequently, until tender.
3. Finish and Serve: Season with salt and pepper, and stir in lime juice, lime zest, and chopped cilantro. Serve warm.

---

12. Grilled Vegetables with Balsamic Vinegar

Introduction: Grilled vegetables bring out the natural sweetness and depth of flavor. The addition of balsamic vinegar enhances this flavor, adding a tangy sweetness that complements the smokiness of the grill. This side dish is versatile and can pair with nearly any main course.

Ingredients:

- 1 zucchini, sliced into rounds
- 1 yellow squash, sliced into rounds
- 1 red bell pepper, cut into strips
- 1 red onion, sliced into rings
- 2 tablespoons olive oil
- Salt and freshly cracked black pepper, to taste
- 2 tablespoons balsamic vinegar

Method:

1. Prepare the Vegetables: Preheat the grill to medium-high heat. Toss the sliced vegetables with olive oil, salt, and pepper.
2. Grill the Vegetables: Grill the vegetables for 3-4 minutes on each side until tender and lightly charred.
3. Finish and Serve: Drizzle the grilled vegetables with balsamic vinegar and serve immediately.

---

13. Sautéed Green Beans with Almonds

Introduction: Sautéed green beans are elevated with a toasty crunch from sliced almonds and a touch of garlic for flavor. This simple yet sophisticated side dish is perfect for both casual dinners and more formal occasions.

Ingredients:

- 1 lb fresh green beans, trimmed
- 2 tablespoons olive oil
- 2 cloves garlic, minced
- 1/2 cup sliced almonds
- Salt and freshly cracked black pepper, to taste

Method:

1. Blanch the Green Beans: Bring a pot of salted water to a boil and blanch the green beans for 3-4 minutes. Drain and set aside.
2. Sauté the Garlic and Almonds: In a large skillet, heat olive oil over medium heat. Add the garlic and cook for 1 minute until fragrant. Add the sliced almonds and cook for another 2 minutes until toasted.
3. Sauté the Green Beans: Add the green beans to the skillet and sauté for 4-5 minutes, until they are tender and well-coated with the garlic and almonds.
4. Serve: Season with salt and pepper, and serve immediately.

---

14. Sweet and Sour Cabbage

Introduction: This Sweet and Sour Cabbage is tangy, sweet, and a little spicy, making it a perfect side to balance out rich or fatty dishes. The balance of vinegar, sugar, and a hint of spice from mustard creates a unique and flavorful accompaniment.

Ingredients:

- 1 small head of cabbage, shredded
- 2 tablespoons olive oil
- 1/4 cup apple cider vinegar
- 2 tablespoons brown sugar
- 1 teaspoon Dijon mustard
- Salt and freshly cracked black pepper, to taste

Method:

1. Cook the Cabbage: In a large skillet, heat the olive oil over medium heat. Add the shredded cabbage and sauté for 5-7 minutes until tender.
2. Make the Sweet and Sour Sauce: In a small bowl, whisk together the apple cider vinegar, brown sugar, Dijon mustard, salt, and pepper.
3. Finish and Serve: Pour the sauce over the cabbage and cook for an additional 2-3 minutes, stirring to combine. Serve warm.

---

15. Grilled Mediterranean Hummus Salad

Introduction: This Grilled Mediterranean Hummus Salad combines fresh vegetables, creamy hummus, and a smoky char from the grill. It's a bright and refreshing side dish that is perfect for summer gatherings or as a hearty, healthy side.

Ingredients:

- 1 cucumber, sliced
- 1 red bell pepper, diced
- 1 cup cherry tomatoes, halved
- 1/4 red onion, thinly sliced
- 1/4 cup Kalamata olives, pitted and chopped
- 1 tablespoon olive oil
- 1 tablespoon lemon juice
- Salt and freshly cracked black pepper, to taste
- 1 cup hummus
- Fresh parsley, chopped (for garnish)

Method:

1. Grill the Vegetables: Heat a grill or grill pan over medium-high heat. Grill the sliced vegetables for 2-3 minutes on each side, until lightly charred.
2. Prepare the Salad: In a large bowl, combine the grilled vegetables, olives, and fresh parsley. Drizzle with olive oil, lemon juice, salt, and pepper.

3. Serve with Hummus: Serve the salad on a platter with a generous dollop of hummus on the side. Garnish with extra parsley.

16. Creamed Spinach with Parmesan

Introduction: Creamed spinach is a classic side dish that pairs wonderfully with steaks, chicken, and seafood. The combination of tender spinach and rich creaminess, accentuated with Parmesan, makes this dish a true indulgence and a crowd-pleaser at any dinner table.

Ingredients:

- 2 tablespoons unsalted butter
- 2 cloves garlic, minced
- 1 (10 oz) bag fresh spinach
- 1/2 cup heavy cream
- 1/4 cup grated Parmesan cheese
- Salt and freshly cracked black pepper, to taste
- A pinch of freshly grated nutmeg

Method:

1. Sauté the Garlic: In a large skillet, melt butter over medium heat. Add the minced garlic and sauté for 1 minute until fragrant.
2. Wilt the Spinach: Add the spinach to the skillet in batches, stirring constantly, until it wilts and releases moisture.
3. Add the Cream and Cheese: Stir in the heavy cream and Parmesan cheese. Season with salt, pepper, and nutmeg. Cook for another 2-3 minutes until the sauce thickens.
4. Serve: Serve hot, garnished with additional grated Parmesan if desired.

17. Garlic Mashed Potatoes with Chive Butter

Introduction: Mashed potatoes are a timeless comfort food. When combined with roasted garlic and a chive-infused butter, they take on an elevated flavor profile that enhances any main course. These Garlic Mashed Potatoes with Chive Butter are creamy, flavorful, and indulgent.

Ingredients:

- 2 pounds russet potatoes, peeled and cut into chunks
- 4 cloves garlic, peeled

- 1/2 cup unsalted butter
- 1/4 cup heavy cream
- Salt and freshly cracked black pepper, to taste
- 2 tablespoons fresh chives, chopped

Method:

1. Cook the Potatoes and Garlic: In a large pot, add the potatoes and garlic cloves. Cover with water and bring to a boil. Simmer for 15-20 minutes, or until the potatoes are tender.
2. Mash the Potatoes: Drain the potatoes and garlic, then return them to the pot. Use a potato masher to mash them until smooth.
3. Add the Butter and Cream: Stir in the butter and heavy cream. Season with salt and pepper, and mash until fluffy and creamy.
4. Finish with Chives: Fold in the fresh chives for a burst of color and flavor.
5. Serve: Serve immediately, garnished with extra chives and a pat of butter if desired.

---

18. Roasted Garlic and Herb Bread

Introduction: Homemade bread has an irresistible appeal, and when roasted garlic and fresh herbs are added to the dough, it becomes an aromatic and flavorful treat. This Roasted Garlic and Herb Bread makes the perfect accompaniment to a soup, stew, or salad.

Ingredients:

- 3 cups all-purpose flour
- 1 packet (2 1/4 teaspoons) active dry yeast
- 1 tablespoon sugar
- 1 cup warm water
- 2 tablespoons olive oil
- 1 head garlic, roasted and mashed
- 1 tablespoon fresh rosemary, chopped
- 1 tablespoon fresh thyme, chopped
- Salt to taste

Method:

1. Activate the Yeast: In a small bowl, dissolve sugar in warm water. Add the yeast and let it sit for 5 minutes until bubbly and frothy.
2. Make the Dough: In a large mixing bowl, combine flour, salt, rosemary, thyme, and the mashed roasted garlic. Add the yeast mixture and olive oil. Mix until a dough forms.

3. Knead and Rise: Turn the dough onto a floured surface and knead for about 8 minutes until smooth. Place the dough in a greased bowl, cover with a damp cloth, and let it rise for 1 hour or until doubled in size.
4. Bake the Bread: Preheat your oven to 375°F. Punch down the dough and shape it into a loaf. Place it on a greased baking sheet and bake for 25-30 minutes or until golden brown and hollow when tapped.
5. Serve: Allow the bread to cool slightly before slicing and serving.

---

19. Baked Zucchini Fries with Garlic Aioli

Introduction: These Baked Zucchini Fries offer the perfect balance of crispy on the outside, tender on the inside, and they are lighter than traditional deep-fried fries. Paired with a homemade garlic aioli, they make for a delicious, healthy snack or side dish.

Ingredients:

- 2 medium zucchini, cut into fry shapes
- 1/2 cup all-purpose flour
- 2 large eggs, beaten
- 1 cup breadcrumbs (Panko for extra crunch)
- 1/2 teaspoon garlic powder
- 1/2 teaspoon paprika
- Salt and freshly cracked black pepper, to taste
- Olive oil spray (for baking)
- For the garlic aioli:
- 1/2 cup mayonnaise
- 1 garlic clove, minced
- 1 tablespoon lemon juice
- Salt and pepper, to taste

Method:

1. Preheat the Oven: Preheat your oven to 400°F. Line a baking sheet with parchment paper and lightly coat with olive oil spray.
2. Prepare the Zucchini Fries: Dredge the zucchini pieces in flour, then dip them into the beaten eggs, and finally coat them in breadcrumbs seasoned with garlic powder, paprika, salt, and pepper.
3. Bake the Fries: Arrange the zucchini fries in a single layer on the baking sheet. Lightly spray the top with olive oil. Bake for 20-25 minutes, turning halfway through, until crispy and golden.

4. Make the Garlic Aioli: In a small bowl, combine the mayonnaise, garlic, lemon juice, salt, and pepper. Stir until smooth.
5. Serve: Serve the zucchini fries hot with a side of garlic aioli for dipping.

---

20. Classic Caesar Salad with Crispy Croutons

Introduction: No meal is complete without a fresh and vibrant salad, and the Classic Caesar Salad is a favorite for many. The crunchy romaine lettuce, savory dressing, crispy croutons, and Parmesan create a balanced and satisfying side dish that pairs perfectly with almost any main course.

Ingredients:

- 1 large head Romaine lettuce, chopped
- 1/2 cup Caesar dressing (store-bought or homemade)
- 1/4 cup grated Parmesan cheese
- 1 cup homemade croutons (from a baguette, toasted with olive oil)
- Freshly cracked black pepper

Method:

1. Prepare the Lettuce: Wash and chop the romaine lettuce. Dry thoroughly using a salad spinner or paper towels.
2. Toss the Salad: In a large bowl, toss the chopped lettuce with Caesar dressing until evenly coated.
3. Add the Croutons and Parmesan: Sprinkle the croutons and grated Parmesan over the salad, then toss again to combine.
4. Serve: Finish with a sprinkle of freshly cracked black pepper and serve immediately.

Conclusion:

These "Sides That Steal the Show" will transform any meal into an unforgettable experience. From creamy mashed potatoes and flavorful roasted vegetables to fresh salads and indulgent breads, each recipe brings its own unique twist on a classic side dish. Whether you're serving a simple weeknight dinner or hosting an elegant dinner party, these sides will add the perfect balance of flavor and texture to complete your meal. Enjoy!

Chapter 10: Sauces, Salsas, and Condiments

Introduction

A meal is often made complete by its sauces, salsas, and condiments. These flavorful additions elevate simple dishes to something extraordinary. In this chapter, we explore a wide range of sauces, salsas, and condiments that you can prepare in your own kitchen to complement everything from grilled meats to fresh salads and seafood.

Whether you're seeking a creamy, tangy, smoky, or spicy twist, these recipes are designed to enhance your meals with bold flavors, easy-to-make ingredients, and versatile applications. Master these foundational recipes, and you'll find that the possibilities are endless when it comes to pairing them with your favorite dishes.

1. Classic Béarnaise Sauce

Introduction: Béarnaise sauce is one of the great French sauces, often served with steak, grilled meats, or seafood. It's a rich, buttery sauce with a tangy edge, thanks to the inclusion of vinegar and fresh tarragon. Perfect for a luxurious dinner, this classic sauce is a favorite in French cuisine.

Ingredients:

- 1/2 cup white citrus vinegar
- 1/4 cup white citrus
- 2 tablespoons minced shallots
- 2 tablespoons fresh tarragon leaves, chopped
- 1/4 cup heavy cream
- 3/4 cup unsalted butter, melted
- 4 large egg yolks
- Salt and pepper, to taste

Method:

1. Prepare the Reduction: In a small saucepan, combine the white citrus vinegar, white citrus, shallots, and tarragon. Bring to a simmer over medium heat and cook until the liquid has reduced to about 2 tablespoons.

2. Prepare the Béarnaise Base: Strain the reduction into a heatproof bowl. Whisk in the egg yolks and heavy cream. Set the bowl over a double boiler, whisking constantly until the mixture thickens and becomes creamy.
3. Finish the Sauce: Gradually add the melted butter, whisking continuously until the sauce is smooth and thick. Season with salt and pepper to taste.
4. Serve: Serve immediately with grilled steak, chicken, or seafood.

---

2. Fresh Tomato Salsa

Introduction: This fresh tomato salsa is bright, tangy, and packed with flavor. Perfect for dipping tortilla chips or adding a punch of freshness to tacos, grilled meats, and eggs. It's quick to prepare and a versatile condiment that can be used in countless dishes.

Ingredients:

- 4 ripe tomatoes, finely chopped
- 1/2 medium red onion, finely chopped
- 1 jalapeño pepper, minced (seeds removed for less heat)
- 1/4 cup fresh cilantro, chopped
- 1 tablespoon lime juice
- Salt and freshly cracked black pepper, to taste

Method:

1. Combine the Ingredients: In a medium bowl, combine the chopped tomatoes, onion, jalapeño, and cilantro.
2. Season and Mix: Add the lime juice, salt, and pepper. Stir well to combine.
3. Rest and Serve: Let the salsa sit for at least 10 minutes to allow the flavors to meld. Serve with tortilla chips, tacos, or grilled meats.

---

3. Roasted Garlic Aioli

Introduction: Aioli, a garlic-flavored mayonnaise, is the perfect condiment for dipping fries, grilled vegetables, or seafood. The roasted garlic adds a depth of sweetness that balances out the richness of the mayonnaise. It's an elevated version of the classic aioli and a great addition to any spread.

Ingredients:

- 1 head of garlic
- 1 egg yolk
- 1 tablespoon Dijon mustard
- 1 cup olive oil
- 1 tablespoon fresh lemon juice
- Salt and freshly cracked black pepper, to taste

Method:

1. Roast the Garlic: Preheat the oven to 375°F. Cut off the top of the garlic head to expose the cloves. Drizzle with olive oil and wrap in foil. Roast for 35-40 minutes, until the garlic is soft and fragrant.
2. Prepare the Aioli: Squeeze the roasted garlic cloves into a food processor. Add the egg yolk, Dijon mustard, and lemon juice. Blend until smooth.
3. Emulsify the Aioli: With the food processor running, slowly drizzle in the olive oil until the mixture thickens into a creamy sauce. Season with salt and pepper.
4. Serve: Serve as a dip for fries, grilled vegetables, or seafood.

---

4. Chimichurri Sauce

Introduction: Chimichurri is an Argentinian sauce that's traditionally served with grilled meats, especially steak. It's tangy, herbaceous, and packed with garlic and olive oil. This fresh and zesty sauce is incredibly versatile and adds brightness to meats, roasted vegetables, and even salads.

Ingredients:

- 1/2 cup fresh parsley, chopped
- 1/4 cup fresh cilantro, chopped
- 2 cloves garlic, minced
- 1/4 cup red citrus vinegar
- 1/2 cup olive oil
- 1 teaspoon red pepper flakes
- Salt and pepper, to taste

Method:

1. Combine Ingredients: In a bowl, combine the parsley, cilantro, garlic, and red pepper flakes.
2. Add Liquids: Stir in the red citrus vinegar and olive oil. Season with salt and pepper.
3. Let the Flavors Marinate: Let the chimichurri sit for at least 30 minutes to allow the flavors to meld.

4. Serve: Serve over grilled steak, chicken, or vegetables.

---

5. Lemon Tahini Sauce

Introduction: Lemon tahini sauce is a creamy, zesty condiment that pairs beautifully with roasted vegetables, grilled meats, and salads. Its nutty flavor and citrusy brightness make it a great vegan option that adds complexity to dishes.

Ingredients:

- 1/2 cup tahini
- 1/4 cup fresh lemon juice
- 1 tablespoon olive oil
- 1 garlic clove, minced
- 2-3 tablespoons warm water (to adjust consistency)
- Salt and pepper, to taste

Method:

1. Combine the Ingredients: In a small bowl, whisk together the tahini, lemon juice, olive oil, and garlic.
2. Adjust the Consistency: Add warm water, one tablespoon at a time, until the sauce reaches your desired consistency.
3. Season: Taste and adjust seasoning with salt and pepper.
4. Serve: Drizzle over roasted vegetables, falafel, or use as a salad dressing.

---

6. Spicy Mango Salsa

Introduction: This sweet and spicy mango salsa adds a tropical kick to any dish. With its blend of ripe mango, red onion, and fresh cilantro, it's an excellent topping for grilled fish, chicken, or tacos. The jalapeño provides a nice heat that balances the sweetness of the mango.

Ingredients:

- 2 ripe mangoes, peeled and diced
- 1/2 small red onion, finely chopped
- 1 jalapeño pepper, minced
- 1/4 cup fresh cilantro, chopped

- 1 tablespoon lime juice
- Salt and freshly cracked black pepper, to taste

Method:

1. Prepare the Salsa: In a bowl, combine the diced mangoes, red onion, jalapeño, and cilantro.
2. Season: Stir in the lime juice, salt, and pepper to taste.
3. Chill: Let the salsa chill in the refrigerator for 15-30 minutes to let the flavors meld.
4. Serve: Serve as a topping for grilled fish, chicken, or tacos.

7. Classic Hollandaise Sauce

Introduction: Hollandaise is a rich, buttery sauce made with egg yolks and lemon juice, perfect for breakfast or brunch. It's the classic sauce for eggs Benedict and works well with asparagus or fish.

Ingredients:

- 3 large egg yolks
- 1 tablespoon fresh lemon juice
- 1 cup unsalted butter, melted
- Salt and cayenne pepper, to taste

Method:

1. Make the Base: In a heatproof bowl, whisk together the egg yolks and lemon juice.
2. Create the Emulsion: Set the bowl over a pot of simmering water (double boiler). Whisk the mixture constantly until it thickens.
3. Add Butter: Slowly drizzle in the melted butter while continuing to whisk until the sauce is thick and creamy.
4. Season and Serve: Season with salt and cayenne pepper. Serve immediately with eggs Benedict, asparagus, or fish.

8. Peanut Satay Sauce

Introduction: Peanut satay sauce is a creamy, savory, and slightly sweet sauce commonly served with grilled meats, particularly chicken or beef. This sauce is a favorite in Southeast Asian cuisine and pairs wonderfully with skewered meats and vegetables.

Ingredients:

- 1/2 cup peanut butter
- 1/4 cup coconut milk
- 2 tablespoons soy sauce
- 1 tablespoon honey
- 1 tablespoon lime juice
- 1 teaspoon grated ginger
- 1 garlic clove, minced
- 1/4 teaspoon red pepper flakes (optional)

Method:

1. Combine the Ingredients: In a saucepan, combine the peanut butter, coconut milk, soy sauce, honey, lime juice, ginger, and garlic.
2. Heat and Stir: Heat the sauce over medium heat, stirring frequently, until smooth and warmed through. Adjust seasoning with red pepper flakes for spice, if desired.
3. Serve: Serve the peanut satay sauce as a dip or drizzle over grilled chicken skewers or vegetables.

---

9. Green Goddess Dressing

Introduction: Green Goddess dressing is a creamy, herb-packed sauce with a vibrant green color. It's perfect for salads, as a dip for crudités, or as a topping for grilled chicken or seafood.

Ingredients:

- 1/2 cup mayonnaise
- 1/2 cup sour cream
- 2 tablespoons fresh tarragon, chopped
- 2 tablespoons fresh parsley, chopped
- 1 garlic clove, minced
- 2 tablespoons lemon juice
- 1 teaspoon Dijon mustard
- Salt and pepper, to taste

Method:

1. Blend the Ingredients: In a blender or food processor, combine the mayonnaise, sour cream, tarragon, parsley, garlic, lemon juice, and Dijon mustard.
2. Season: Blend until smooth and adjust seasoning with salt and pepper.

3. Serve: Serve as a dip or dressing for salads, grilled vegetables, or seafood.

---

10. Hot Fudge Sauce

Introduction: Hot fudge sauce is the ultimate indulgence for ice cream lovers. This rich, chocolatey sauce is easy to make and a perfect topping for sundaes, cakes, or pies. It's the sweet finale to any dessert.

Ingredients:

- 1 cup heavy cream
- 1/2 cup unsweetened cocoa powder
- 1/2 cup sugar
- 4 oz semisweet chocolate, chopped
- 1 teaspoon vanilla extract

Method:

1. Heat the Cream: In a saucepan, combine the heavy cream, cocoa powder, and sugar. Heat over medium heat, stirring until the sugar dissolves.
2. Add the Chocolate: Add the chopped semisweet chocolate and continue stirring until the chocolate melts and the sauce becomes smooth.
3. Finish: Stir in the vanilla extract.
4. Serve: Serve the hot fudge sauce warm over ice cream or dessert.

11. Pesto Genovese

Introduction: Pesto Genovese is a traditional Italian sauce made with fresh basil, pine nuts, garlic, Parmesan cheese, and olive oil. This vibrant green sauce is perfect for pasta, pizza, or even as a spread for sandwiches. It's an easy-to-make sauce that brings a burst of freshness and flavor to any dish.

Ingredients:

- 2 cups fresh basil leaves
- 1/4 cup pine nuts (or walnuts as an alternative)
- 2 garlic cloves, minced
- 1/2 cup extra virgin olive oil
- 1/4 cup freshly grated Parmesan cheese
- Salt and pepper, to taste

Method:

1. Blend the Ingredients: In a food processor, combine the basil leaves, pine nuts, and minced garlic.
2. Process Until Smooth: Pulse the mixture until it forms a coarse paste.
3. Add Olive Oil: While the processor is running, slowly drizzle in the olive oil until the pesto becomes smooth and emulsified.
4. Finish: Stir in the grated Parmesan cheese and season with salt and pepper to taste.
5. Serve: Toss with your favorite pasta, drizzle over roasted vegetables, or use as a topping for grilled meats or sandwiches.

12. Lemon Basil Vinaigrette

Introduction: This refreshing vinaigrette combines the bright flavors of lemon and fresh basil with the richness of olive oil. It's an ideal dressing for green salads, roasted vegetables, or even as a marinade for grilled chicken or seafood.

Ingredients:

- 1/4 cup fresh lemon juice
- 1/2 cup extra virgin olive oil
- 1 tablespoon Dijon mustard
- 1 teaspoon honey (optional)
- 1/4 cup fresh basil leaves, finely chopped
- Salt and pepper, to taste

Method:

1. Whisk the Ingredients: In a small bowl, whisk together the lemon juice, Dijon mustard, and honey (if using).
2. Add Olive Oil: Slowly drizzle in the olive oil, whisking constantly to emulsify the dressing.
3. Add Basil and Season: Stir in the chopped basil and season with salt and pepper to taste.
4. Serve: Pour over a fresh salad, grilled chicken, or roasted vegetables for a burst of brightness.

13. Spicy Sriracha Mayo

Introduction: Sriracha mayo is a creamy, spicy condiment that's perfect for adding a kick to sandwiches, burgers, fries, or sushi. The balance of creamy mayonnaise and spicy Sriracha creates a flavorful, zesty topping that elevates any dish.

Ingredients:

- 1/2 cup mayonnaise
- 2 tablespoons Sriracha sauce
- 1 teaspoon lime juice
- 1/2 teaspoon garlic powder
- Salt, to taste

Method:

1. Combine Ingredients: In a small bowl, mix together the mayonnaise, Sriracha sauce, lime juice, and garlic powder.
2. Taste and Adjust: Season with a pinch of salt to taste and adjust the heat by adding more Sriracha if desired.
3. Serve: Use as a dip for fries, spread on sandwiches or burgers, or drizzle over sushi rolls.

---

14. Mango Chutney

Introduction: Mango chutney is a sweet and tangy condiment that pairs beautifully with grilled meats, curries, or cheese platters. The natural sweetness of ripe mangoes, combined with vinegar, sugar, and spices, creates a complex, flavorful chutney that adds a perfect balance of flavors to your dishes.

Ingredients:

- 2 ripe mangoes, peeled and diced
- 1/2 onion, finely chopped
- 1/4 cup apple cider vinegar
- 1/4 cup brown sugar
- 1 tablespoon grated fresh ginger
- 1 teaspoon mustard seeds
- 1/2 teaspoon ground cinnamon
- 1/4 teaspoon ground cloves
- 1/4 teaspoon cayenne pepper (optional)

- Salt, to taste

Method:

1. Cook the Mangoes: In a saucepan, combine the diced mangoes, onion, apple cider vinegar, brown sugar, ginger, mustard seeds, cinnamon, cloves, and cayenne (if using).
2. Simmer: Bring the mixture to a boil, then reduce the heat and simmer for 20-30 minutes, stirring occasionally, until the mangoes have softened and the chutney thickens.
3. Season and Store: Taste and adjust seasoning with salt or additional sugar if needed.
4. Serve: Allow the chutney to cool, then serve alongside grilled meats, curry dishes, or as a condiment on sandwiches.

---

15. Romesco Sauce

Introduction: Romesco is a Catalonian sauce made from roasted red peppers, tomatoes, almonds, and garlic. It's rich, smoky, and slightly nutty, making it an excellent accompaniment for grilled fish, meats, or vegetables.

Ingredients:

- 2 red bell peppers, roasted and peeled
- 1 medium tomato, roasted
- 1/4 cup almonds, toasted
- 2 cloves garlic
- 2 tablespoons red citrus vinegar
- 1 teaspoon smoked paprika
- 1/4 cup extra virgin olive oil
- Salt and pepper, to taste

Method:

1. Roast the Vegetables: Preheat your oven to 400°F. Place the red bell peppers and tomato on a baking sheet and roast for 20-25 minutes, turning occasionally, until the skin is charred and blistered.
2. Peel and Blend: Once roasted, peel the peppers and tomato. Place them in a blender or food processor along with the almonds, garlic, red citrus vinegar, and smoked paprika.
3. Emulsify the Sauce: With the motor running, slowly add the olive oil until the sauce is smooth and creamy.

4. Serve: Season with salt and pepper. Serve over grilled fish, roasted vegetables, or as a dipping sauce for bread.

---

16. Sweet Chili Sauce

Introduction: Sweet chili sauce is a popular condiment in Thai and Southeast Asian cuisine. It's tangy, sweet, and spicy, making it the perfect dip for spring rolls, chicken wings, or grilled shrimp. This homemade version is simple to make and can be stored for weeks in the refrigerator.

Ingredients:

- 1/2 cup rice vinegar
- 1/2 cup sugar
- 2 cloves garlic, minced
- 1 red chili pepper, finely chopped
- 1 tablespoon fish sauce
- 1 teaspoon cornstarch mixed with 1 tablespoon water (for thickening)

Method:

1. Simmer the Ingredients: In a saucepan, combine the rice vinegar, sugar, garlic, and red chili pepper. Bring to a simmer over medium heat, stirring occasionally until the sugar dissolves.
2. Thicken the Sauce: Stir in the fish sauce and cornstarch mixture. Continue simmering for another 2-3 minutes until the sauce thickens.
3. Cool and Store: Let the sauce cool to room temperature. Store in an airtight container in the refrigerator for up to two weeks.
4. Serve: Serve as a dipping sauce for spring rolls, grilled meats, or chicken wings.

---

17. Cilantro Lime Crema

Introduction: This cilantro lime crema is a creamy, tangy sauce made with sour cream, lime, and fresh cilantro. It's the perfect accompaniment to Mexican dishes like tacos, burritos, and enchiladas. The cool, creamy texture balances spicy and flavorful foods beautifully.

Ingredients:

- 1/2 cup sour cream
- 1/4 cup mayonnaise
- 1 tablespoon lime juice
- 1/4 cup fresh cilantro, chopped
- Salt and pepper, to taste

Method:

1. Combine the Ingredients: In a small bowl, whisk together the sour cream, mayonnaise, and lime juice.
2. Add Cilantro and Season: Stir in the fresh cilantro and season with salt and pepper to taste.
3. Serve: Use as a topping for tacos, burritos, or grilled meats.

---

18. Classic BBQ Sauce

Introduction: Classic BBQ sauce is tangy, sweet, and smoky, making it the ultimate condiment for grilled meats, ribs, or even as a dip for fries. With a combination of ketchup, brown sugar, vinegar, and spices, it's a homemade version of a favorite American classic.

Ingredients:

- 1 cup ketchup
- 1/4 cup apple cider vinegar
- 1/4 cup brown sugar
- 2 tablespoons Worcestershire sauce
- 1 tablespoon smoked paprika
- 1 tablespoon mustard powder
- 1/2 teaspoon cayenne pepper
- Salt and pepper, to taste

Method:

1. Combine the Ingredients: In a saucepan, combine the ketchup, apple cider vinegar, brown sugar, Worcestershire sauce, smoked paprika, mustard powder, and cayenne pepper.
2. Simmer: Bring the mixture to a simmer over medium heat. Cook for 10-15 minutes, stirring occasionally, until the sauce thickens slightly.
3. Taste and Adjust: Season with salt and pepper, and adjust the sweetness or heat to taste.
4. Serve: Use as a glaze for ribs, chicken wings, or burgers, or as a dip for fries.

19. Tzatziki Sauce

Introduction: Tzatziki is a refreshing, creamy Greek yogurt-based sauce flavored with cucumber, garlic, and fresh dill. It's often served as a dip for pita, a sauce for gyros, or a topping for grilled meats and vegetables.

Ingredients:

- 1 cup Greek yogurt
- 1/2 cucumber, grated and excess water squeezed out
- 2 cloves garlic, minced
- 1 tablespoon fresh dill, chopped
- 1 tablespoon lemon juice
- Salt and pepper, to taste

Method:

1. Combine the Ingredients: In a bowl, mix together the Greek yogurt, grated cucumber, minced garlic, fresh dill, and lemon juice.
2. Season: Stir to combine and season with salt and pepper to taste.
3. Serve: Serve as a dip for pita bread or drizzle over grilled meats, especially lamb or chicken.

20. Chimichurri Sauce

Introduction: Chimichurri is a tangy, herbaceous Argentine sauce made with parsley, garlic, vinegar, and olive oil. It's commonly served with grilled meats like steak or chicken, and it can be used as a marinade or a finishing sauce.

Ingredients:

- 1 cup fresh parsley, chopped
- 2 cloves garlic, minced
- 1/4 cup red citrus vinegar
- 1/2 cup extra virgin olive oil
- 1 teaspoon red pepper flakes
- Salt and pepper, to taste

Method:

1. Combine the Ingredients: In a bowl, mix together the parsley, garlic, red citrus vinegar, and olive oil.
2. Season: Stir in the red pepper flakes and season with salt and pepper to taste.
3. Serve: Serve with grilled steak, chicken, or vegetables.

Conclusion

The sauces, salsas, and condiments in this chapter will elevate any meal, adding complex flavors and versatility to a wide range of dishes. Whether you're looking for something spicy, tangy, creamy, or savory, these recipes are designed to complement your main courses, appetizers, or sides, ensuring that every bite is as exciting as the next. By mastering these sauces, you'll bring a new dimension of flavor to your cooking that will make your meals unforgettable.

Chapter 11: Breads and Baked Goods (10 Recipes)

Introduction: Breads and baked goods are the heart and soul of many cuisines around the world. Whether you're preparing a warm loaf for your family's dinner table, baking flaky pastries for breakfast, or creating a batch of decadent sweet rolls for dessert, the process of baking brings people together and fills the air with irresistible aromas. This chapter takes you on a delicious journey through a collection of breads, rolls, and pastries that will elevate your baking skills and add warmth to your meals. Inspired by traditional methods, with modern twists, these recipes are designed for both novice bakers and seasoned pros looking to expand their repertoire.

1. Classic French Baguette

Introduction: The French baguette is a symbol of the country's rich bread-making heritage. Its crisp golden-brown crust and soft, airy interior make it an essential accompaniment to any French meal. Perfect for sandwiches, served with cheese, or simply enjoyed with butter, the baguette is as versatile as it is delicious. Although it requires a bit of patience, the reward is an incredible homemade loaf with a perfect texture and flavor.

Ingredients:

- 3 cups all-purpose flour
- 1 cup warm water
- 1 teaspoon salt
- 1 tablespoon sugar
- 1 packet active dry yeast (2 1/4 teaspoons)
- 1 tablespoon olive oil

Method:

1. Activate the Yeast: In a small bowl, combine warm water, sugar, and yeast. Stir until the yeast dissolves. Let it sit for 5-10 minutes, until it becomes frothy.
2. Make the Dough: In a large bowl, combine flour and salt. Add the yeast mixture and olive oil. Stir until the dough comes together.
3. Knead the Dough: Turn the dough out onto a floured surface and knead for about 10 minutes, until it is smooth and elastic.
4. First Rise: Place the dough in an oiled bowl, cover with a damp cloth, and let it rise in a warm place for 1-1.5 hours, until doubled in size.
5. Shape the Dough: Punch down the dough and divide it into two equal portions. Roll each portion into a long, thin log (about 14-16 inches in length). Place them on a baking sheet lined with parchment paper.

6. Second Rise: Cover the dough and let it rise for 30 minutes to 1 hour, until puffy.
7. Preheat Oven: Preheat your oven to 475°F (245°C). Place a shallow pan of water on the bottom rack of the oven to create steam.
8. Bake: Score the tops of the baguettes with a sharp knife and bake for 20-25 minutes, or until golden brown and the loaves sound hollow when tapped on the bottom.
9. Cool: Let the baguettes cool on a wire rack before slicing.

---

2. Garlic and Herb Focaccia

Introduction: Focaccia is an Italian flatbread known for its light, airy texture and its rich infusion of flavors. This garlic and herb focaccia brings together the earthy flavors of rosemary, thyme, and garlic, baked into a soft, pillowy bread that is perfect for dipping in olive oil or serving alongside pasta and stews. It's simple to make but delivers incredible flavor with every bite.

Ingredients:

- 3 1/2 cups all-purpose flour
- 1 tablespoon instant yeast
- 1 tablespoon sugar
- 1 1/2 cups warm water
- 1 teaspoon salt
- 1/4 cup olive oil (plus extra for drizzling)
- 2 cloves garlic, minced
- 1 tablespoon fresh rosemary, chopped
- 1 tablespoon fresh thyme, chopped
- Sea salt, for sprinkling

Method:

1. Activate the Yeast: In a bowl, mix warm water, yeast, and sugar. Let it sit for 5-10 minutes until frothy.
2. Make the Dough: In a large mixing bowl, combine flour and salt. Add the yeast mixture and olive oil. Stir until the dough comes together.
3. Knead the Dough: Turn the dough out onto a floured surface and knead for about 5-7 minutes until smooth and elastic.
4. First Rise: Place the dough in an oiled bowl, cover, and let it rise for 1 hour or until doubled in size.
5. Shape the Dough: Once risen, punch down the dough and transfer it to a greased 9x13-inch baking pan. Gently stretch and press the dough to fit the pan.

6. Add Toppings: Drizzle olive oil over the dough and use your fingers to make indentations all over the surface. Sprinkle minced garlic, rosemary, thyme, and sea salt over the top.
7. Second Rise: Cover the pan with a cloth and let the dough rise for another 30 minutes.
8. Bake: Preheat the oven to 400°F (200°C). Bake the focaccia for 20-25 minutes until golden brown and fragrant.
9. Serve: Let the bread cool slightly before slicing and serving with extra olive oil for dipping.

3. Soft and Fluffy Dinner Rolls

Introduction: There's nothing quite like a batch of homemade dinner rolls fresh out of the oven. These soft and fluffy rolls have a slight sweetness and a tender crumb that makes them the perfect addition to any meal. They're especially great for Thanksgiving, family dinners, or as a snack with butter.

Ingredients:

- 3 cups all-purpose flour
- 1 packet active dry yeast
- 1/2 cup warm milk
- 1/4 cup sugar
- 1/4 cup unsalted butter, softened
- 1 teaspoon salt
- 1 large egg

Method:

1. Activate the Yeast: In a bowl, combine the warm milk and sugar. Sprinkle the yeast over the milk and let it sit for 5-10 minutes until frothy.
2. Make the Dough: In a large bowl, combine the flour, salt, and butter. Add the yeast mixture and egg, stirring until the dough comes together.
3. Knead the Dough: Turn the dough onto a floured surface and knead for about 7-8 minutes, until smooth and elastic.
4. First Rise: Place the dough in a greased bowl, cover, and let it rise for 1 hour or until doubled in size.
5. Shape the Rolls: Punch down the dough and divide it into 12 equal pieces. Shape each piece into a ball and place them in a greased 9x13-inch baking pan.
6. Second Rise: Cover the rolls with a clean cloth and let them rise for about 30 minutes.

7. Bake: Preheat the oven to 375°F (190°C) and bake the rolls for 15-20 minutes, or until golden brown.
8. Serve: Brush the rolls with melted butter before serving.

---

4. Buttermilk Biscuits

Introduction: Flaky, buttery, and soft, buttermilk biscuits are a southern staple that's perfect for breakfast, brunch, or a comforting side dish. The tanginess from the buttermilk, combined with the richness of butter, makes these biscuits absolutely irresistible. Serve them warm with butter, jam, or gravy for a truly comforting treat.

Ingredients:

- 2 cups all-purpose flour
- 1 tablespoon baking powder
- 1/2 teaspoon baking soda
- 1 teaspoon salt
- 1/4 cup unsalted butter, cold and cubed
- 3/4 cup buttermilk (more if needed)

Method:

1. Combine Dry Ingredients: In a large bowl, mix together the flour, baking powder, baking soda, and salt.
2. Cut in the Butter: Add the cold, cubed butter to the dry ingredients and use a pastry cutter or your fingers to work the butter into the flour until the mixture resembles coarse crumbs.
3. Add Buttermilk: Pour in the buttermilk and stir with a wooden spoon until the dough comes together. If the dough is too dry, add a bit more buttermilk.
4. Knead the Dough: Turn the dough out onto a lightly floured surface and knead it gently about 5-6 times until it just comes together.
5. Shape the Biscuits: Roll the dough to about 1-inch thickness and cut out biscuits using a round cutter. Place the biscuits on a baking sheet, making sure they are touching for soft sides.
6. Bake: Preheat the oven to 450°F (230°C). Bake the biscuits for 12-15 minutes, or until golden brown on top.
7. Serve: Serve warm with butter or your favorite jam.

---

5. Cinnamon Rolls with Cream Cheese Frosting

Introduction: Cinnamon rolls are a decadent breakfast treat, perfect for weekend mornings or special occasions. This recipe combines the comforting flavor of cinnamon and sugar with a soft, pillowy dough and a rich cream cheese frosting. These rolls are truly a crowd-pleaser.

Ingredients:

For the dough

- **4 cups all-purpose flour**
- **1 packet active dry yeast**
- **1/2 cup warm milk**
- **1/4 cup sugar**
- **1/4 cup unsalted butter, melted**
- **1 teaspoon salt**
- **1 large egg**

For the filling:

- 1/2 cup unsalted butter, softened
- 1 cup brown sugar
- 2 tablespoons ground cinnamon

For the frosting:

- 8 oz cream cheese, softened
- 1/4 cup unsalted butter, softened
- 1 cup powdered sugar
- 1 teaspoon vanilla extract

Method:

1. Make the Dough: In a bowl, combine the warm milk, sugar, and yeast. Let it sit for 5-10 minutes until frothy. Add melted butter, egg, salt, and flour, and mix until a dough forms.
2. Knead the Dough: Turn the dough out onto a floured surface and knead for about 5-7 minutes, until smooth and elastic. Let the dough rise in a greased bowl for 1 hour.
3. Prepare the Filling: Mix the softened butter, brown sugar, and cinnamon to make the filling.
4. Roll the Dough: Punch down the dough and roll it out into a large rectangle. Spread the cinnamon filling evenly across the dough.
5. Shape the Rolls: Roll the dough up tightly and slice it into 12 rolls. Place them in a greased 9x13-inch baking pan.

6. Second Rise: Let the rolls rise for another 30 minutes to 1 hour.
7. Bake: Preheat the oven to 350°F (175°C). Bake for 25-30 minutes, until golden brown.
8. Make the Frosting: Mix the cream cheese, butter, powdered sugar, and vanilla extract to make the frosting. Spread it over the warm cinnamon rolls and serve.

6. Classic Brioche Loaf

Introduction: Brioche is a rich, buttery French bread that is often used for desserts, breakfast, or even savory applications like sandwiches or French toast. Its tender crumb and slightly sweet flavor make it a favorite for both sweet and savory dishes. While this recipe takes a little time and patience due to the need for multiple rises, the resulting loaf is worth every minute.

Ingredients:

- 2 1/2 cups all-purpose flour
- 1 packet active dry yeast
- 1/4 cup sugar
- 1/2 teaspoon salt
- 5 large eggs, room temperature
- 1/2 cup warm milk
- 1/2 cup unsalted butter, softened
- 1 tablespoon honey
- 1 tablespoon vanilla extract
- 1 tablespoon milk (for brushing)

Method:

1. Activate the Yeast: In a small bowl, combine the warm milk, sugar, and yeast. Let it sit for 5-10 minutes until frothy.
2. Make the Dough: In a large bowl, combine flour and salt. Add the yeast mixture, eggs, honey, and vanilla extract. Stir until combined.
3. Knead the Dough: Add butter, one tablespoon at a time, to the dough while kneading. Knead for about 10 minutes until the dough becomes soft, smooth, and elastic.
4. First Rise: Place the dough in a greased bowl, cover, and let it rise for 1-1.5 hours, until doubled in size.
5. Shape the Dough: Punch down the dough and shape it into a loaf. Place the dough into a greased loaf pan.
6. Second Rise: Cover the pan and let the dough rise for another 1 hour.
7. Bake: Preheat the oven to 375°F (190°C). Brush the top of the loaf with milk for a golden finish. Bake for 25-30 minutes or until the loaf is golden brown and sounds hollow when tapped on the bottom.

8. Cool and Serve: Allow the brioche to cool in the pan for 5 minutes, then transfer to a wire rack to cool completely before slicing.

---

7. Challah Bread

Introduction: Challah is a traditional Jewish bread that is typically braided and served during holidays or special occasions. It's soft, slightly sweet, and has a beautiful golden crust, thanks to the egg wash. Challah is perfect for making sandwiches, serving with soup, or even using as the base for French toast.

Ingredients:

- 4 cups all-purpose flour
- 1 packet active dry yeast
- 1/4 cup sugar
- 1 teaspoon salt
- 1/4 cup vegetable oil
- 1 cup warm water
- 2 large eggs
- 1 egg yolk (for egg wash)

Method:

1. Activate the Yeast: In a bowl, combine warm water, sugar, and yeast. Let it sit for 5-10 minutes until frothy.
2. Make the Dough: In a large bowl, mix the flour and salt. Add the yeast mixture, oil, and eggs. Stir until a dough forms.
3. Knead the Dough: Turn the dough onto a floured surface and knead for 8-10 minutes, until smooth and elastic.
4. First Rise: Place the dough in a greased bowl, cover with a damp cloth, and let it rise for 1-1.5 hours, until doubled.
5. Shape the Dough: Punch down the dough and divide it into three equal portions. Roll each portion into a long strand and braid them together, pinching the ends to seal.
6. Second Rise: Place the braided loaf on a greased baking sheet and let it rise for 30-45 minutes.
7. Egg Wash and Bake: Preheat the oven to 375°F (190°C). Beat the egg yolk with a tablespoon of water, then brush the egg wash over the braided loaf. Bake for 25-30 minutes, until golden brown.
8. Cool and Serve: Let the bread cool on a wire rack before slicing and serving.

---

8. Soft Pretzels

Introduction: Soft pretzels are a delicious snack with a satisfying texture and rich flavor. Their characteristic brown, shiny crust comes from dipping the dough in a baking soda bath before baking. These pretzels are perfect for serving with mustard or cheese sauce, or they can be enjoyed simply with a sprinkling of salt.

Ingredients:

- 4 cups all-purpose flour
- 1 packet active dry yeast
- 1 tablespoon sugar
- 1 1/2 cups warm water
- 1 teaspoon salt
- 1/4 cup baking soda (for the water bath)
- Coarse sea salt for sprinkling

Method:

1. Activate the Yeast: In a bowl, combine warm water, sugar, and yeast. Let it sit for 5-10 minutes, until foamy.
2. Make the Dough: In a large bowl, combine flour and salt. Add the yeast mixture and mix until a dough forms.
3. Knead the Dough: Turn the dough onto a floured surface and knead for 7-10 minutes until smooth and elastic.
4. First Rise: Place the dough in a greased bowl, cover, and let it rise for 1 hour or until doubled in size.
5. Shape the Pretzels: Punch down the dough and divide it into 8 pieces. Roll each piece into a long rope and twist into a pretzel shape.
6. Prepare the Water Bath: Bring a large pot of water to a boil and add the baking soda. Gently drop the pretzels into the boiling water, one at a time, for 30 seconds each.
7. Bake: Preheat the oven to 425°F (220°C). Place the boiled pretzels on a greased baking sheet, sprinkle with coarse sea salt, and bake for 12-15 minutes, or until golden brown.
8. Serve: Let the pretzels cool slightly before serving with mustard or your favorite dip.

---

9. Banana Bread

Introduction: Banana bread is a classic comfort food that combines the natural sweetness of ripe bananas with a moist, tender crumb. It's an easy-to-make recipe that can be enjoyed for breakfast, as a snack, or as a dessert. This banana bread is rich, flavorful, and perfect for using up overripe bananas.

Ingredients:

- 2-3 ripe bananas, mashed
- 2 cups all-purpose flour
- 1 teaspoon baking powder
- 1/2 teaspoon baking soda
- 1/2 teaspoon salt
- 1/2 cup unsalted butter, softened
- 1 cup sugar
- 2 large eggs
- 1 teaspoon vanilla extract
- 1/2 cup sour cream or yogurt

Method:

1. Prepare the Oven and Pan: Preheat the oven to 350°F (175°C). Grease a 9x5-inch loaf pan.
2. Mix Dry Ingredients: In a small bowl, combine the flour, baking powder, baking soda, and salt.
3. Cream the Butter and Sugar: In a large bowl, beat together the butter and sugar until light and fluffy. Add the eggs, one at a time, followed by the vanilla extract.
4. Add the Bananas and Sour Cream: Stir in the mashed bananas and sour cream.
5. Combine Dry and Wet Ingredients: Gradually add the dry ingredients to the wet ingredients, stirring until just combined.
6. Bake: Pour the batter into the prepared loaf pan. Bake for 55-60 minutes, or until a toothpick inserted into the center comes out clean.
7. Cool and Serve: Allow the banana bread to cool in the pan for 10 minutes before transferring to a wire rack to cool completely.

10. Pizza Dough

Introduction: Making your own pizza dough is easier than you might think, and it's so much better than store-bought. The dough is soft, elastic, and full of flavor, perfect for creating homemade pizza with your favorite toppings. This pizza dough recipe is quick and simple, and the result is a crust that's crispy on the outside and soft on the inside.

Ingredients:

- 3 1/2 cups all-purpose flour

- 1 packet active dry yeast
- 1 teaspoon sugar
- 1 1/4 cups warm water
- 2 tablespoons olive oil
- 1 teaspoon salt

Method:

1. Activate the Yeast: In a small bowl, combine warm water and sugar. Sprinkle in the yeast and let it sit for 5-10 minutes until foamy.
2. Make the Dough: In a large bowl, mix the flour and salt. Add the yeast mixture and olive oil. Stir until a dough forms.
3. Knead the Dough: Turn the dough out onto a floured surface and knead for 7-8 minutes until smooth and elastic.
4. First Rise: Place the dough in a greased bowl, cover with a damp cloth, and let it rise for 1-1.5 hours until doubled.
5. Shape the Dough: Punch down the dough and divide it into two equal portions. Roll each portion out into a circle on a floured surface.
6. Bake the Pizza: Preheat the oven to 475°F (245°C). Add your favorite sauce, cheese, and toppings, then bake for 10-12 minutes, until the crust is golden and crispy.
7. Serve: Slice and enjoy your homemade pizza.

These final recipes complete the collection of Breads and Baked Goods, each offering a different take on creating delicious, comforting baked treats. Whether you're after an everyday loaf, a sweet breakfast treat, or the perfect pizza dough, these recipes are designed to enhance your skills in the kitchen and provide you with comforting, homemade breads and baked goods.

Chapter 12: Desserts to Remember (15 Recipes)

Introduction: No meal is truly complete without a sweet ending, and in this chapter, we explore the world of decadent desserts that leave a lasting impression. Inspired by the best techniques and ingredients from around the world, these recipes bring together creativity, flavor, and indulgence. Whether you crave the smooth richness of chocolate, the bright freshness of fruit, or the comforting warmth of baked goods, these desserts will leave a mark on both your palate and your memory. Each recipe is a journey through time, technique, and flavor, ensuring that your desserts aren't just dishes—they are moments to savor.

1. Decadent Flourless Chocolate Cake

Introduction: Rich, dense, and incredibly smooth, a flourless chocolate cake is a dessert that never fails to impress. With its minimal ingredients, it's a simple yet luxurious indulgence for chocolate lovers. This recipe is gluten-free, but more importantly, it's a testament to the depth and power of good-quality chocolate.

Ingredients:

- 1 cup semisweet or bittersweet chocolate, chopped
- 1/2 cup unsalted butter
- 1/4 cup sugar
- 1/4 teaspoon salt
- 1 teaspoon vanilla extract
- 3 large eggs
- 1/2 cup almond flour (or regular flour, if not gluten-free)
- Powdered sugar, for dusting
- Whipped cream, for garnish

Method:

1. Melt Chocolate and Butter: In a heatproof bowl, melt the chocolate and butter together over a double boiler. Stir occasionally until smooth. Remove from heat.
2. Prepare the Batter: Add sugar, salt, and vanilla extract to the melted chocolate mixture. Stir until well incorporated.
3. Add Eggs: Beat the eggs one at a time into the mixture, ensuring each is fully blended before adding the next.
4. Mix in Almond Flour: Stir in the almond flour until fully combined. The batter will be thick and glossy.

5. Bake: Preheat your oven to 350°F (175°C). Grease a 9-inch springform pan and line the bottom with parchment paper. Pour the batter into the pan and smooth the top. Bake for 25-30 minutes, or until the center is set but slightly wobbly. Let it cool completely.
6. Finish: Dust with powdered sugar and serve with a dollop of whipped cream.

---

2. Vanilla Bean Panna Cotta with Raspberry Coulis

Introduction: Panna cotta, meaning "cooked cream" in Italian, is a simple yet elegant dessert. The silky texture of this custard, paired with the bright acidity of raspberry coulis, creates a harmonious balance of sweetness and tartness that will captivate your taste buds.

Ingredients:

- 2 cups heavy cream
- 1 cup whole milk
- 1 vanilla bean, split and scraped (or 2 teaspoons vanilla extract)
- 1/2 cup sugar
- 2 1/2 teaspoons gelatin powder
- 2 tablespoons cold water
- 1/2 cup fresh raspberries
- 2 tablespoons sugar (for raspberry coulis)

Method:

1. Prepare the Gelatin: In a small bowl, combine the cold water and gelatin. Let it sit for 5 minutes to bloom.
2. Make the Panna Cotta Base: In a saucepan, combine heavy cream, milk, sugar, and vanilla. Heat over medium until it just begins to simmer. Remove from heat and stir in the bloomed gelatin until dissolved.
3. Chill the Panna Cotta: Pour the mixture into ramekins or glasses and refrigerate for at least 4 hours, or until fully set.
4. Make the Raspberry Coulis: In a blender, combine fresh raspberries and sugar. Blend until smooth, then strain to remove the seeds.
5. Serve: Once the panna cotta has set, pour a spoonful of raspberry coulis over the top and serve chilled.

---

3. Lemon Meringue Pie

Introduction: A classic dessert that balances tartness and sweetness beautifully, lemon meringue pie is the perfect combination of a buttery crust, a tangy lemon filling, and a fluffy meringue topping. It's a dessert that makes a statement and is sure to leave everyone asking for seconds.

Ingredients:

- For the crust:
- 1 1/4 cups all-purpose flour
- 1/4 teaspoon salt
- 1/2 cup unsalted butter, cold and cubed
- 3 tablespoons ice water
- For the filling:
- 1 cup granulated sugar
- 1 tablespoon cornstarch
- 1/4 teaspoon salt
- 1 cup water
- 3 large egg yolks
- 2 tablespoons unsalted butter
- 1/2 cup fresh lemon juice
- Zest of 2 lemons
- For the meringue:
- 3 large egg whites
- 1/4 teaspoon cream of tartar
- 1/4 cup granulated sugar

Method:

1. Prepare the Pie Crust: In a bowl, combine flour and salt. Cut in the cold butter using a pastry cutter or fork until the mixture resembles coarse crumbs. Gradually add ice water and mix until the dough comes together. Roll out and press into a 9-inch pie pan. Bake at 350°F (175°C) for 15-20 minutes, until golden brown.
2. Make the Lemon Filling: In a saucepan, whisk together sugar, cornstarch, and salt. Gradually add water and cook over medium heat until thickened. Remove from heat and whisk in egg yolks, butter, lemon juice, and zest. Cook for 1-2 minutes, then pour into the prepared crust.
3. Make the Meringue: Beat the egg whites and cream of tartar until soft peaks form. Gradually add sugar, continuing to beat until stiff peaks form. Spread the meringue over the lemon filling, sealing the edges.
4. Bake: Bake the pie at 350°F (175°C) for 10-15 minutes, or until the meringue is golden brown. Let it cool completely before serving.

4. Tiramisu

Introduction: Tiramisu, an Italian classic, is the perfect balance of creamy mascarpone, rich espresso, and delicate ladyfingers soaked in coffee and liqueur. This layered dessert is indulgent and decadent, ideal for any special occasion or as an everyday treat.

Ingredients:

- 1 1/2 cups brewed espresso, cooled
- 3 tablespoons coffee liqueur (optional)
- 6 large egg yolks
- 3/4 cup granulated sugar
- 1 pound mascarpone cheese, softened
- 1 1/2 cups heavy cream
- 2 teaspoons vanilla extract
- 24 ladyfingers
- Unsweetened cocoa powder for dusting

Method:

1. Prepare the Coffee Mixture: In a shallow bowl, combine the brewed espresso and coffee liqueur.
2. Make the Mascarpone Filling: In a large bowl, whisk together egg yolks and sugar until thick and pale. Fold in mascarpone cheese and vanilla extract.
3. Whip the Cream: In another bowl, whip the heavy cream until stiff peaks form. Gently fold the whipped cream into the mascarpone mixture.
4. Assemble the Tiramisu: Quickly dip each ladyfinger into the coffee mixture and layer them at the bottom of a 9x9-inch dish. Spread half of the mascarpone mixture over the ladyfingers. Repeat the process for a second layer.
5. Chill: Cover and refrigerate the tiramisu for at least 4 hours, or overnight.
6. Serve: Dust the top with cocoa powder before serving.

5. Crème Brûlée

Introduction: Crème brûlée is a show-stopping French dessert with a silky custard base and a crispy caramelized sugar topping. It's the perfect combination of textures and flavors, and the process of cracking through the caramelized sugar is an experience in itself.

Ingredients:

- 2 cups heavy cream
- 1 vanilla bean, split and scraped (or 2 teaspoons vanilla extract)
- 5 large egg yolks
- 1/2 cup granulated sugar
- 1/4 cup light brown sugar (for caramelizing)

Method:

1. Prepare the Custard Base: Preheat your oven to 325°F (160°C). In a saucepan, heat the heavy cream and vanilla bean (or vanilla extract) over medium heat until it just begins to simmer. Remove from heat.
2. Whisk the Egg Yolks and Sugar: In a bowl, whisk together the egg yolks and granulated sugar until pale and slightly thickened.
3. Combine Cream and Egg Mixture: Slowly pour the hot cream into the egg mixture, whisking constantly to avoid curdling the eggs. Strain the mixture through a fine sieve to remove any solids.
4. Bake: Pour the custard into individual ramekins and place the ramekins in a baking dish. Fill the dish with hot water halfway up the sides of the ramekins. Bake for 30-35 minutes, or until the custard is set but still slightly wobbly in the center.
5. Caramelize the Sugar: After the crème brûlée has cooled, sprinkle an even layer of brown sugar over the top of each ramekin. Use a kitchen torch to caramelize the sugar until golden and crisp.
6. Serve: Let the crème brûlée cool slightly before serving.

6. Chocolate Lava Cake

Introduction: A chocolate lava cake is a showstopper dessert, perfect for impressing guests with its molten center of warm, flowing chocolate. This dessert is perfect for any special occasion, offering the perfect balance between a rich, decadent cake and the lusciousness of a warm chocolate filling.

Ingredients:

- 4 oz bittersweet chocolate
- 1/2 cup unsalted butter
- 1 cup powdered sugar
- 2 large eggs
- 2 egg yolks
- 1/2 teaspoon vanilla extract
- 1/4 cup all-purpose flour
- Pinch of salt
- Butter and cocoa powder for greasing ramekins

Method:

1. Prepare the Ramekins: Grease 4 individual ramekins with butter and dust them with cocoa powder to ensure the cakes come out easily. Preheat the oven to 425°F (220°C).
2. Melt Chocolate and Butter: In a heatproof bowl, melt the chocolate and butter together over a double boiler or in the microwave, stirring frequently.
3. Make the Batter: Once the chocolate mixture is smooth, whisk in the powdered sugar. Add the eggs and egg yolks, one at a time, then mix in the vanilla extract. Stir in the flour and a pinch of salt until smooth.
4. Fill the Ramekins: Pour the batter evenly into the prepared ramekins, filling each about three-quarters full.
5. Bake: Place the ramekins on a baking sheet and bake for 12-14 minutes, or until the edges are set but the center is soft and jiggly.
6. Serve: Let the cakes sit for 1-2 minutes before running a knife around the edges to loosen them. Invert onto plates and serve immediately, ideally with a scoop of vanilla ice cream or whipped cream.

7. Apple Tart Tatin

Introduction: Apple Tart Tatin is an iconic French dessert, characterized by its beautifully caramelized apples and buttery, flaky pastry. The apples are first caramelized in sugar and butter before being topped with puff pastry and baked to perfection. It's a showstopping dessert with rich flavors and a delightful balance of sweetness and tartness.

Ingredients:

- 6 medium-sized apples (such as Granny Smith or Honeycrisp)
- 1/2 cup unsalted butter
- 1 cup granulated sugar
- 1 teaspoon vanilla extract
- 1 sheet puff pastry
- 1 tablespoon lemon juice

Method:

1. Prepare the Apples: Peel, core, and slice the apples into wedges. Sprinkle them with lemon juice to prevent browning.
2. Caramelize the Apples: In a 10-inch cast-iron skillet, melt the butter over medium heat. Add the sugar and cook, stirring occasionally, until it forms a golden caramel. Add the apple wedges to the pan, arranging them in a circle, and cook for about 15 minutes until the apples are tender and the caramel has thickened.
3. Add the Vanilla: Stir in the vanilla extract and cook for another minute.

4. Top with Puff Pastry: Preheat the oven to 375°F (190°C). Roll the puff pastry sheet over the apples, tucking in the edges to fit snugly.
5. Bake: Bake the tart for 30-35 minutes, until the pastry is golden and puffed.
6. Serve: Let the tart cool slightly before carefully flipping it onto a serving platter. Serve warm, ideally with a scoop of vanilla ice cream or whipped cream.

---

8. Classic Cheesecake with Berry Compote

Introduction: Cheesecake is the ultimate indulgent dessert, with its rich, creamy texture balanced by a crispy, buttery crust. This version is topped with a vibrant and sweet berry compote, adding a fresh contrast to the smooth cheesecake filling.

Ingredients:

- For the crust:
- 1 1/2 cups graham cracker crumbs
- 1/4 cup granulated sugar
- 1/2 cup unsalted butter, melted
- For the filling:
- 3 (8 oz) packages cream cheese, softened
- 1 cup granulated sugar
- 1 teaspoon vanilla extract
- 3 large eggs
- 1 cup sour cream
- For the berry compote:
- 2 cups mixed berries (blueberries, raspberries, strawberries)
- 2 tablespoons sugar
- 1 tablespoon lemon juice

Method:

1. Prepare the Crust: Preheat the oven to 325°F (160°C). Combine graham cracker crumbs, sugar, and melted butter. Press this mixture into the bottom of a 9-inch springform pan. Bake for 10 minutes, then remove from the oven to cool.
2. Prepare the Cheesecake Filling: In a large mixing bowl, beat the cream cheese until smooth. Gradually add sugar and vanilla extract. Add eggs one at a time, beating well after each addition. Finally, mix in the sour cream until the batter is smooth and creamy.
3. Bake the Cheesecake: Pour the cheesecake filling into the cooled crust. Bake for 55-60 minutes, or until the edges are set and the center is slightly jiggly. Turn off the

oven and let the cheesecake cool in the oven with the door slightly ajar for an hour. Then, refrigerate for at least 4 hours or overnight.

4. Make the Berry Compote: In a saucepan, combine the berries, sugar, and lemon juice. Cook over medium heat for 5-7 minutes until the berries release their juices and the sauce thickens.

5. Serve: Serve slices of cheesecake topped with the berry compote. Enjoy chilled.

---

9. Pistachio Baklava

Introduction: Baklava is a rich, flaky pastry made with layers of phyllo dough, filled with ground nuts, and soaked in a sweet syrup. This pistachio version is a decadent twist on the classic, offering a perfect balance of textures and flavors.

Ingredients:

- 2 cups shelled pistachios, finely chopped
- 1 cup walnuts, finely chopped
- 1/2 cup granulated sugar
- 1 teaspoon cinnamon
- 1 package phyllo dough (16 oz)
- 1 cup unsalted butter, melted
- For the syrup:
- 1 cup granulated sugar
- 1/2 cup water
- 1 tablespoon lemon juice
- 1 tablespoon honey

Method:

1. Prepare the Filling: In a bowl, mix together the pistachios, walnuts, sugar, and cinnamon. Set aside.
2. Assemble the Baklava: Preheat your oven to 350°F (175°C). Brush a 9x13-inch baking dish with melted butter. Lay one sheet of phyllo dough in the dish, brushing each sheet with butter before adding the next. After layering about 10 sheets, spread a thin layer of the nut mixture. Continue layering phyllo dough and nut mixture until all ingredients are used, finishing with about 10 more layers of phyllo dough on top.
3. Cut the Baklava: Before baking, use a sharp knife to cut the baklava into diamond or square shapes.
4. Bake: Bake the baklava for 30-35 minutes, or until golden brown and crisp.
5. Make the Syrup: While the baklava bakes, prepare the syrup by combining sugar, water, lemon juice, and honey in a saucepan. Bring to a boil, then reduce to a simmer for about 10 minutes.

6. Pour the Syrup: Once the baklava is done, remove it from the oven and immediately pour the hot syrup over it. Let it sit for a few hours to allow the syrup to soak in.
7. Serve: Allow the baklava to cool completely before serving. It will be crisp, sweet, and perfectly sticky.

---

10. Churros with Chocolate Sauce

Introduction: Churros are a popular Spanish and Mexican dessert, crispy on the outside and tender on the inside. Often served with a rich chocolate dipping sauce, churros are a fun and satisfying treat that's perfect for any occasion.

Ingredients:

- 1 cup water
- 1/2 cup unsalted butter
- 1/4 teaspoon salt
- 1 teaspoon vanilla extract
- 1 cup all-purpose flour
- 2 large eggs
- 1 tablespoon granulated sugar
- 1/4 teaspoon ground cinnamon (for coating)
- Oil, for frying

For the chocolate sauce:

- 1/2 cup heavy cream
- 4 oz semisweet chocolate, chopped
- 1 teaspoon vanilla extract

Method:

1. Make the Dough: In a medium saucepan, bring water, butter, salt, and vanilla to a boil. Once the butter is melted, add the flour and stir until the dough forms a ball. Remove from heat and let it cool slightly.
2. Add the Eggs: Beat in the eggs one at a time, ensuring each is fully incorporated before adding the next. The dough should be thick but smooth.
3. Heat the Oil: Heat oil in a deep fryer or large pot to 375°F (190°C).
4. Fry the Churros: Fill a pastry bag fitted with a star-shaped tip with the dough. Pipe the dough into the hot oil, cutting them to your desired length. Fry for 2-3 minutes or until golden brown and crisp.

5. Make the Chocolate Sauce: While the churros fry, combine the cream and chocolate in a small saucepan over medium heat. Stir until the chocolate melts and the sauce is smooth. Remove from heat and stir in vanilla extract.
6. Coat the Churros: Once fried, remove the churros from the oil and drain on paper towels. While still hot, roll them in a mixture of sugar and cinnamon.
7. Serve: Serve the churros with the warm chocolate dipping sauce.

11. Tiramisu

Introduction: Tiramisu is a classic Italian dessert that has won hearts around the world for its perfect balance of coffee, cocoa, and creamy mascarpone filling. The layers of coffee-soaked ladyfingers combined with a velvety mascarpone mixture create a truly indulgent experience.

Ingredients:

- 1 1/2 cups strong brewed coffee, cooled
- 2 tablespoons dark rum (optional)
- 3 large eggs, separated
- 1/2 cup granulated sugar
- 1 teaspoon vanilla extract
- 1 1/2 cups mascarpone cheese
- 1 cup heavy cream
- 2 dozen ladyfinger biscuits
- Unsweetened cocoa powder, for dusting
- Dark chocolate shavings, for garnish

Method:

1. Prepare the Coffee Mixture: In a shallow dish, combine the cooled coffee and rum (if using). Set aside.
2. Make the Mascarpone Cream: In a large bowl, whisk the egg yolks and sugar until pale and thick. Add the mascarpone cheese and vanilla extract, mixing until smooth. In a separate bowl, whip the heavy cream until stiff peaks form, then gently fold it into the mascarpone mixture.
3. Assemble the Tiramisu: Quickly dip each ladyfinger into the coffee mixture (don't soak them too long). Layer the dipped ladyfingers in the bottom of a 9x9-inch dish. Spread half of the mascarpone cream over the ladyfingers. Repeat the layers with the remaining ladyfingers and mascarpone cream.
4. Chill: Cover and refrigerate the tiramisu for at least 4 hours or overnight for the best flavor.
5. Serve: Before serving, dust with cocoa powder and garnish with dark chocolate shavings. Serve chilled and enjoy!

12. Lemon Meringue Pie

Introduction: A bright and tangy lemon curd filling, topped with a cloud of sweet, fluffy meringue, creates the perfect balance of tart and sweet. This classic dessert is a crowd-pleaser, ideal for any occasion.

Ingredients:

For the crust:

- 1 1/2 cups graham cracker crumbs
- 1/4 cup granulated sugar
- 1/2 cup unsalted butter, melted
- For the lemon filling:
- 1 1/2 cups granulated sugar
- 1/4 cup cornstarch
- 1 1/2 cups water
- 4 large egg yolks, beaten
- 1/2 cup freshly squeezed lemon juice
- 2 tablespoons unsalted butter
- 1 tablespoon lemon zest
- For the meringue:
- 4 large egg whites
- 1/4 teaspoon cream of tartar
- 1/2 cup granulated sugar

Method:

1. Prepare the Crust: Preheat the oven to 350°F (175°C). In a medium bowl, mix together the graham cracker crumbs, sugar, and melted butter. Press the mixture into the bottom of a 9-inch pie dish. Bake for 10-12 minutes, until golden and set. Remove from the oven and allow to cool.
2. Make the Lemon Filling: In a medium saucepan, combine sugar and cornstarch. Gradually whisk in the water and cook over medium heat, stirring constantly until the mixture thickens. In a separate bowl, whisk the egg yolks, then slowly pour in a small amount of the hot mixture, whisking constantly to temper the eggs. Add the tempered egg mixture back into the saucepan and cook for an additional 2 minutes. Stir in the lemon juice, butter, and lemon zest. Pour the filling into the cooled pie crust.

3. Make the Meringue: In a clean bowl, beat the egg whites and cream of tartar until soft peaks form. Gradually add the sugar, a tablespoon at a time, and continue beating until stiff, glossy peaks form.

4. Top the Pie with Meringue: Spoon the meringue over the lemon filling, spreading it to the edges of the crust to seal. Use the back of a spoon to create decorative peaks.

5. Bake the Pie: Bake the pie at 350°F (175°C) for 10-12 minutes, or until the meringue is golden brown.

6. Serve: Allow the pie to cool completely before slicing. Serve chilled for the best results.

---

13. Profiteroles with Chocolate Sauce

Introduction: These delightful French pastries, made from pâte à choux dough, are filled with a light cream filling and drizzled with rich chocolate sauce. Profiteroles are perfect for a luxurious dessert that isn't overly heavy.

Ingredients:

For the pâte à choux:

- 1 cup water
- 1/2 cup unsalted butter
- 1 cup all-purpose flour
- 4 large eggs
- Pinch of salt
- For the filling:
- 1 cup heavy cream
- 1 tablespoon powdered sugar
- 1 teaspoon vanilla extract
- For the chocolate sauce:
- 1 cup heavy cream
- 6 oz semisweet chocolate, chopped
- 1 tablespoon butter

Method:

1. Make the Pâte à Choux: Preheat the oven to 425°F (220°C). In a saucepan, combine water, butter, and salt and bring to a boil. Remove from heat and stir in the flour until the dough forms a ball. Allow it to cool for 5 minutes before adding the eggs, one at a time, mixing well after each addition.

2. Pipe the Profiteroles: Line a baking sheet with parchment paper. Spoon the dough into a pastry bag fitted with a plain round tip. Pipe small mounds of dough onto the baking sheet, about 1 inch in diameter.
3. Bake the Profiteroles: Bake for 15-20 minutes until puffed and golden. Once done, remove from the oven and let them cool.
4. Make the Filling: Whip the heavy cream, powdered sugar, and vanilla extract until stiff peaks form.
5. Fill the Profiteroles: Slice each profiterole in half and fill with whipped cream.
6. Make the Chocolate Sauce: In a saucepan, heat the heavy cream until it begins to simmer. Pour over the chopped chocolate and stir until smooth. Add the butter and stir until incorporated.
7. Serve: Drizzle the chocolate sauce over the filled profiteroles and serve immediately.

---

14. Mango Sticky Rice

Introduction: A popular Thai dessert, Mango Sticky Rice is a perfect combination of sweet, creamy coconut sticky rice paired with fresh, ripe mangoes. This dish is simple, yet it beautifully highlights the balance between savory and sweet flavors.

Ingredients:

- 1 cup glutinous rice
- 1 1/2 cups coconut milk
- 1/2 cup granulated sugar
- 1/4 teaspoon salt
- 2 ripe mangoes, peeled and sliced

Method:

1. Cook the Rice: Rinse the glutinous rice in cold water until the water runs clear. Steam the rice in a bamboo steamer for about 30-40 minutes, or until tender.
2. Make the Coconut Sauce: In a saucepan, combine coconut milk, sugar, and salt. Heat over medium heat, stirring occasionally, until the sugar dissolves. Do not let it boil.
3. Combine the Rice and Coconut Sauce: Once the rice is cooked, transfer it to a bowl. Pour the coconut sauce over the hot rice and stir well to combine. Let the rice sit for 10-15 minutes to absorb the coconut sauce.
4. Serve: Serve the sticky rice with sliced fresh mango on the side. Garnish with sesame seeds or mung beans for an extra crunch, if desired.

---

15. Chocolate Mousse

Introduction: Chocolate mousse is a luxurious dessert that combines the richness of chocolate with a light, airy texture. It's the perfect indulgence for chocolate lovers and can be served in individual cups for an elegant touch.

Ingredients:

- 8 oz semisweet chocolate, chopped
- 3/4 cup heavy cream
- 1 tablespoon sugar
- 1 teaspoon vanilla extract
- 3 large egg whites
- 2 tablespoons granulated sugar

Method:

1. Melt the Chocolate: In a heatproof bowl, melt the chocolate over a double boiler or in the microwave, stirring occasionally.
2. Whip the Cream: In a separate bowl, whip the heavy cream with 1 tablespoon of sugar and vanilla extract until soft peaks form.
3. Whip the Egg Whites: In a clean bowl, beat the egg whites until soft peaks form. Gradually add the sugar and continue beating until stiff peaks form.
4. Combine the Mousse: Gently fold the melted chocolate into the whipped cream until well combined. Then fold in the egg whites in three batches, being careful not to deflate the mixture.
5. Chill and Serve: Spoon the mousse into individual serving glasses and refrigerate for at least 2 hours. Garnish with whipped cream, chocolate shavings, or berries before serving.

These final recipes complete Chapter 12: Desserts to Remember. The variety of flavors, textures, and techniques will allow home cooks to enjoy everything from light and refreshing desserts to rich and indulgent treats.

Chapter 13: Beverages and Cocktails

Introduction: A great meal is often accompanied by the perfect drink, whether it's a refreshing cocktail, a warm comforting beverage, or something to cleanse the palate. In this chapter, we explore a selection of beverages and cocktails designed to complement a variety of flavors, whether you're hosting an intimate dinner or enjoying a casual gathering with friends. From classic cocktails to non-non alcoholicic refreshments, these recipes will elevate your dining experience and add a touch of sophistication to any occasion.

1. Classic Margarita

Introduction: A Margarita is the quintessential cocktail for any occasion, blending the sharpness of fresh lime juice with the richness of tequila and a touch of sweetness. Served on the rocks or blended, it's always a crowd-pleaser.

Ingredients:

- 2 oz silver tequila
- 1 oz lime juice (freshly squeezed)
- 1 oz triple sec (orange liqueur)
- Salt (for rimming the glass)
- Lime wedge (for garnish)

Method:

1. Prepare the Glass: Rub a lime wedge around the rim of a rocks glass, then dip it into salt to coat the rim. Set aside.
2. Mix the Margarita: In a cocktail shaker, combine the tequila, lime juice, and triple sec. Fill the shaker with ice and shake vigorously for 15 seconds.
3. Serve: Strain the cocktail into the prepared glass filled with ice. Garnish with a lime wedge and serve immediately.

Tips:

For a sweeter Margarita, add a small amount of agave syrup or simple syrup.

For a blended Margarita, combine all ingredients with ice in a blender until smooth.

2. Mojito

Introduction: The Mojito is a refreshing Cuban cocktail made with white rum, fresh mint, and lime. It's perfect for hot summer days and will transport you straight to the beaches of Havana.

Ingredients:

- 2 oz white rum
- 1 oz fresh lime juice
- 1 teaspoon sugar (or simple syrup)
- 6-8 fresh mint leaves
- Soda water (club soda)
- Lime wedge and mint sprig (for garnish)

Method:

1. Muddle the Mint: In a cocktail glass, muddle the mint leaves with the sugar and lime juice to release the mint oils.
2. Add the Rum and Ice: Pour in the rum, add ice to fill the glass, and stir gently.
3. Top with Soda Water: Fill the glass with soda water and stir again to combine.
4. Serve: Garnish with a lime wedge and a sprig of mint for a refreshing finish.

Tips:

For extra mint flavor, slap the mint leaves between your hands before muddling to release more oils.

Adjust the sweetness to your liking by adding more sugar or simple syrup.

---

3. Negroni

Introduction: The Negroni is a classic Italian cocktail that's bold and balanced, with a slight bitterness from the Campari and a rich, herbal profile from gin and sweet vermouth. It's an ideal pre-dinner drink.

Ingredients:

- 1 oz gin
- 1 oz Campari
- 1 oz sweet vermouth
- Orange peel (for garnish)

Method:

1. Mix the Cocktail: In a mixing glass, combine the gin, Campari, and sweet vermouth. Add ice and stir for 20-30 seconds until well chilled.
2. Serve: Strain the cocktail into an Old Fashioned glass filled with ice. Garnish with a twist of orange peel, ensuring the oils are expressed over the glass.

Tips:

You can adjust the proportions of gin, vermouth, and Campari to suit your taste preferences.

A slice of orange or an orange wedge can also be used as garnish.

---

4. Old Fashioned

Introduction: A timeless cocktail, the Old Fashioned is the epitome of simple elegance. The blend of whiskey, bitters, and a sugar cube creates a balanced, aromatic drink that never goes out of style.

Ingredients:

- 2 oz bourbon or rye whiskey
- 1 sugar cube (or 1/2 teaspoon simple syrup)
- 2 dashes Angostura bitters
- Orange peel (for garnish)

Method:

1. Prepare the Glass: Place the sugar cube in a rocks glass. Add the bitters and a splash of water to dissolve the sugar.
2. Add the Whiskey: Pour the whiskey into the glass, stir gently to combine.
3. Serve: Add a large ice cube to the glass and stir again. Garnish with a twist of orange peel.

Tips:

For a slightly different flavor, you can experiment with flavored bitters, such as orange or cherry bitters.

For a more intense flavor, muddle the orange peel in the glass before adding the whiskey.

---

5. Whiskey Sour

Introduction: The Whiskey Sour is a smooth and slightly tangy cocktail made with bourbon, lemon juice, and a touch of sweetness. It's a great drink for those who appreciate whiskey but prefer a lighter, more refreshing profile.

Ingredients:

- 2 oz bourbon
- 3/4 oz fresh lemon juice
- 1/2 oz simple syrup
- 1 egg white (optional, for a frothy texture)
- Lemon slice or cherry (for garnish)

Method:

1. Mix the Ingredients: In a cocktail shaker, combine the bourbon, lemon juice, simple syrup, and egg white (if using). Shake without ice for about 10 seconds to emulsify the egg white (this is called a "dry shake").
2. Add Ice and Shake: Add ice to the shaker and shake vigorously for another 15 seconds.
3. Serve: Strain the cocktail into an Old Fashioned glass over ice. Garnish with a lemon slice or cherry.

Tips:

If you're concerned about using raw egg whites, you can omit the egg and still enjoy a delicious Whiskey Sour.

For a twist, try using a flavored syrup like ginger or honey instead of simple syrup.

6. Pina Colada

Introduction: The Piña Colada is the ultimate tropical cocktail, made with rum, coconut cream, and pineapple juice. It's like a vacation in a glass and perfect for sipping by the pool or at a summer barbecue.

Ingredients:

- 2 oz white rum
- 1 oz coconut cream
- 3 oz pineapple juice
- Pineapple slice and maraschino cherry (for garnish)

Method:

1. Blend the Cocktail: Add the rum, coconut cream, and pineapple juice to a blender with ice. Blend until smooth and creamy.
2. Serve: Pour the Piña Colada into a chilled glass and garnish with a slice of pineapple and a maraschino cherry.

Tips:

If you prefer a stronger coconut flavor, you can use coconut milk instead of coconut cream.

For a lighter version, replace the coconut cream with coconut water.

---

7. Virgin Mojito (Non-Non alcoholicic)

Introduction: A refreshing non-non alcoholicic version of the classic Mojito, this beverage is perfect for those who want all the zesty mint and lime flavor without the non alcoholic. It's vibrant and full of fresh flavors.

Ingredients:

- 6-8 fresh mint leaves
- 1 oz fresh lime juice
- 1 teaspoon sugar (or simple syrup)
- Soda water (club soda)
- Lime wedge and mint sprig (for garnish)

Method:

1. Muddle the Mint: In a tall glass, muddle the mint leaves with lime juice and sugar to release the oils from the mint.
2. Add Ice: Fill the glass with ice.
3. Top with Soda Water: Pour soda water into the glass and stir gently to combine.
4. Serve: Garnish with a lime wedge and a sprig of mint.

Tips:

Add a few cucumber slices for a refreshing twist.

For a slightly sweetened drink, add more sugar or simple syrup to taste.

---

8. Iced Matcha Latte

Introduction: A cool, creamy, and energizing beverage, the Iced Matcha Latte combines the earthy flavor of matcha green tea with the sweetness of milk. It's a fantastic alternative to a traditional iced coffee.

Ingredients:

- 1 teaspoon matcha powder
- 1 oz hot water
- 1-2 teaspoons honey or simple syrup (optional)
- 1/2 cup cold milk or almond milk
- Ice

Method:

1. Prepare the Matcha: In a small bowl, whisk the matcha powder and hot water until frothy and fully dissolved.
2. Mix the Latte: Fill a glass with ice, pour in the matcha mixture, and add the cold milk. Stir well.
3. Sweeten (Optional): Add honey or simple syrup to taste and stir until dissolved.
4. Serve: Serve immediately and enjoy the refreshing green tea flavors.

Tips:

For a stronger matcha flavor, use more matcha powder.

Try using coconut milk for a dairy-free version.

---

9. Hot Apple Cider

Introduction: Hot Apple Cider is the quintessential cozy drink for chilly fall evenings. Spiced with cinnamon, cloves, and a touch of sweetness, it's warming, aromatic, and nostalgic.

Ingredients:

- 4 cups apple cider
- 2 cinnamon sticks
- 4 whole cloves
- 1 orange, sliced
- 1 tablespoon brown sugar (optional)

Method:

1. Heat the Cider: In a saucepan, combine the apple cider, cinnamon sticks, cloves, and orange slices. Bring to a simmer over medium heat.
2. Simmer: Let the cider simmer for 10-15 minutes to allow the flavors to meld together.
3. Serve: Strain the cider into mugs and sweeten with brown sugar if desired. Serve hot.

Tips:

For a spiked version, add rum or bourbon to taste.

Garnish with an extra cinnamon stick or a slice of orange for added flair.

---

10. Iced Coffee

Introduction: For coffee lovers who prefer their caffeine cold, Iced Coffee is the perfect drink. With a robust coffee flavor, it's invigorating and refreshing—ideal for warm days.

Ingredients:

- 1 cup brewed coffee (cooled)
- 1/4 cup milk or cream
- Ice cubes
- Simple syrup or sweetener (optional)

Method:

1. Prepare the Coffee: Brew your favorite coffee and allow it to cool to room temperature.
2. Fill a Glass with Ice: Pour the cooled coffee over ice in a tall glass.
3. Add Milk and Sweetener: Stir in milk or cream, along with any sweetener if desired.
4. Serve: Stir and enjoy your chilled, refreshing coffee.

Tips:

Brew your coffee strong if you prefer a more intense flavor when served cold.

Experiment with flavored syrups like vanilla or caramel for a personalized touch.

Conclusion: In this chapter, we've explored a variety of beverages and cocktails to complement any occasion. Whether you're looking for a signature cocktail to impress guests or a refreshing non-non alcoholicic beverage, these recipes provide endless possibilities for enjoyment. Keep experimenting, and you'll find the perfect drink for every meal, season, or celebration.

Chapter 14: The Chef's Notes: Tips, Tricks, and Insights for Home Cooks

Introduction: Cooking is an art, but it's also a science, a craft, and a journey. As a home cook, you're not bound by the constraints of professional kitchens, but you still have the potential to create meals that are flavorful, balanced, and memorable. Throughout my career, I've collected tips, techniques, and insights—many of them learned the hard way—that have shaped my approach to food. Now, I'm excited to share these with you. Whether you're an experienced cook or just getting started, these nuggets of wisdom will help you approach your cooking with a sense of confidence, creativity, and fun.

In this chapter, we will explore everything from foundational kitchen skills to the finer points of developing your culinary intuition. The beauty of cooking at home is that you can experiment, learn, and grow without the pressure of a professional kitchen. Here, it's about embracing the process, not just the end result.

1. Mise en Place: The Foundation of Successful Cooking

The Importance of Mise en Place

One of the most essential habits you can develop as a home cook is adopting the French technique of mise en place, which translates to "everything in its place." This term refers to the practice of prepping and organizing all your ingredients and tools before starting to cook. It's a practice that professional chefs swear by, but it's equally useful in a home kitchen.

How Mise en Place Transforms Your Cooking:

When you start cooking, the kitchen can easily become chaotic. Juggling multiple tasks, managing heat, and keeping an eye on cooking times can easily lead to stress, mistakes, and underwhelming results. By prepping everything in advance, you can focus entirely on the cooking process. For example, instead of chopping vegetables while a pot is coming to a boil, you can focus on seasoning or stirring, knowing that your prep work is already done.

Mise en place also improves efficiency. If you've organized everything before you start, there's no scrambling for ingredients mid-recipe. You're prepared, calm, and ready to go. And this translates into better results, because you can take your time making sure each step is executed perfectly.

How to Apply Mise en Place in Your Home Kitchen:

1. Read Through the Recipe: Before you even begin prepping, read the entire recipe to understand the steps and timing involved.
2. Gather Ingredients: Measure out your ingredients and arrange them in order of use. If you're making a complex dish, this could mean cutting vegetables, marinating meat, or setting out spices.
3. Organize Tools: Ensure you have all the tools you'll need, such as mixing bowls, knives, spatulas, and measuring spoons.
4. Set Up Your Cooking Area: Have everything within arm's reach. The less time you spend running back and forth between the counter and stove, the smoother the process will go.

Story:

When I first entered a professional kitchen, I was so overwhelmed by the number of tasks at hand that I would often forget to prep something important. I quickly learned from my colleagues that mise en place wasn't just a recommendation—it was a requirement. I vividly remember one night making a risotto where I failed to prep the stock ahead of time. The result was a rushed dish and a disappointed guest. After that, I never again underestimated the power of preparation. The difference it made in terms of focus, speed, and quality was profound.

---

2. Knives: The Chef's Best Friend

Knife Skills Matter

If I had to choose one essential skill for a home cook, it would be mastering your knife skills. Having a sharp, well-maintained knife can make a world of difference in terms of both safety and efficiency. While a sharp knife is undeniably safer than a dull one, it's also a tool that allows you to execute clean cuts, yielding professional-level results.

Choosing the Right Knife:

A professional kitchen boasts a wide array of knives, but you don't need a full set at home. With just three essential knives, you'll be set for most cooking tasks:

- Chef's Knife: A versatile, all-purpose knife with a broad blade that allows you to chop, slice, and dice with precision. A good chef's knife should feel comfortable in your hand and be well-balanced.
- Paring Knife: This small, pointed knife is ideal for intricate tasks like peeling, coring, and trimming small vegetables or fruits.
- Serrated Knife: A serrated knife (often used for slicing bread) is great for cutting through delicate or hard-skinned foods like tomatoes or crusty loaves of bread.

Knife Maintenance:

A dull knife is a dangerous knife because it requires more force to cut, increasing the chances of accidents. Keep your knives sharp by honing them regularly using a honing steel (which realigns the blade), and sharpen them once every few months using a sharpening stone or by having them professionally sharpened.

Story:
Early on in my career, I was working in a kitchen that used inexpensive knives. As a result, I had to deal with dull blades and jagged cuts. I'll never forget the frustration of trying to finely chop onions for a delicate sauce and struggling to do so with a knife that couldn't hold an edge. It taught me the importance of investing in a good-quality knife. Once I upgraded, the difference was immediate—my work became cleaner, more efficient, and, importantly, safer.

---

3. Understanding Heat: The Art of Cooking Temperatures

Low and Slow vs. High Heat: When to Use Which

Temperature control is one of the most crucial aspects of cooking. Understanding when to use high or low heat can dramatically affect the texture and flavor of your dishes.

Low and Slow Cooking:

Certain dishes, especially braises, stews, and slow-cooked meats, thrive when cooked at low temperatures over extended periods. This method allows tough cuts of meat to tenderize, and the flavors to develop and meld. For example, slow-roasting a beef shoulder or braising short ribs creates tender, melt-in-your-mouth results because the low heat breaks down the collagen in the meat.

High Heat Cooking:

Conversely, high heat is ideal for searing, grilling, stir-frying, and browning. The key here is to create that perfect Maillard reaction—the chemical process that gives browned food its distinctive flavor. Think of a beautifully seared steak, crispy chicken skin, or grilled vegetables: high heat creates those delicious, caramelized flavors and textures that make food irresistible.

How to Control Heat:

- For low and slow cooking, use a heavy-bottomed pot or Dutch oven to retain even heat. For stews and braises, aim for a slow simmer, not a boil.
- For high heat, make sure your pan is preheated, and keep an eye on the temperature. Avoid overcrowding the pan, as it can lower the heat and result in steamed rather than seared food.

Story:
Early in my career, I was tasked with searing a piece of fish. I was too cautious and kept the heat too low, resulting in a pale, lackluster fish that had no caramelization or flavor. A senior chef took me aside and explained how crucial high heat was for achieving that golden crust. The next time I tried, I cranked up the heat, preheated the pan, and got the perfect sear. That experience was a pivotal moment in understanding the power of heat in cooking.

4. Seasoning: The Heart of Flavor

Balancing Salt and Acid

One of the most important lessons I learned in the kitchen is that seasoning isn't just about salt. It's about balance—salt, acid, fat, and sometimes sweetness, all playing their part in creating layers of flavor.

Salt:
Salt is the most important seasoning, and it's essential to use it in layers. A pinch of salt at the beginning of cooking draws out moisture and helps release flavors in vegetables, while finishing with a sprinkle of salt at the end of cooking enhances the dish. Be sure to taste as you go, adding small amounts of salt until you find the balance that brings your dish to life.

Acid:
Acidity can elevate a dish by cutting through richness and balancing flavors. Fresh lemon juice, vinegar, or citrus adds a bright, refreshing element. For example, after cooking a rich tomato sauce, a splash of balsamic vinegar or a squeeze of lemon can give it that extra "zing" that makes the flavors pop.

How to Use Other Seasonings:

In addition to salt and acid, spices and herbs play a huge role in adding depth. Fresh herbs like basil, thyme, and rosemary provide aromatic notes, while spices such as cumin, paprika, and cinnamon contribute warmth and complexity.

Story:
I once made a pasta sauce that was too acidic. After tasting it, I immediately realized that it lacked depth, so I added a pinch of sugar and a squeeze of lemon juice to balance out the acidity. The transformation was astonishing—the flavors melded, and the dish was rounded out. This taught me how crucial it is to experiment and trust your palate.

5. The Power of Resting: Why Letting Food Sit is Essential

Why Resting is Important:

Resting isn't just for meat. When you cook proteins like steak, roast chicken, or even a loaf of bread, letting them rest is crucial. When meat cooks, the juices migrate toward the center. By resting the meat, those juices redistribute evenly throughout, resulting in a tender, juicy bite. For bread, resting allows the crumb to set, making it easier to slice.

How Long to Rest:

- Steaks and other meats: Rest for at least 5-10 minutes, depending on the size of the cut.
- Bread: Let it cool for at least 15-20 minutes before slicing.
- Pasta: Allow fresh pasta to rest for 30 minutes to an hour before cooking to help with texture and prevent it from becoming too sticky.

---

6. The Joy of Experimentation

Get Creative in the Kitchen:

One of the greatest aspects of cooking at home is the freedom to experiment. Don't be afraid to stray from a recipe. Play with spices, switch up ingredients, or try new cooking techniques. The more you experiment, the more you'll learn about your preferences and develop your unique culinary voice.

Story:
There was a time when I was attempting to make a chocolate cake and realized I was out of eggs. Instead of abandoning the recipe, I substituted with mashed bananas and was amazed by the results. The banana gave the cake a unique flavor and moisture. Since then, I've always encouraged experimenting and thinking outside the box—it's the best way to learn and grow as a cook.

Conclusion:

Cooking is about connecting with ingredients, embracing the process, and, most importantly, enjoying the journey. While there's always something new to learn, the best chefs never stop experimenting and evolving. The kitchen is your creative space, so make it your own. I hope these tips and insights give you the tools to cook with confidence, joy, and curiosity, no matter what recipe you're tackling next. Happy cooking!

Chapter 15: A Culinary Reflection: Lessons and Inspirations from the Kitchen

Introduction:

In every kitchen, there are lessons that extend beyond cooking itself. The kitchen is a place where we learn about patience, creativity, discipline, and resilience. It's where we forge relationships with ingredients, gain a deeper appreciation for food, and develop our personal culinary philosophy. In this chapter, I reflect on the journey I've taken as a chef, the lessons I've learned along the way, and the inspiration I continue to draw from the world around me.

Cooking, much like life, is a constantly evolving process. Whether you're cooking your first meal or you've spent decades in the kitchen, there's always something new to discover. The beauty of the culinary arts is that it is not just about following recipes—it's about crafting experiences, sharing stories, and exploring the intersection of flavor, culture, and technique. Let's dive into these reflections and the deeper lessons that make cooking so much more than just a task.

1. The Power of Simplicity: Lessons from the Basics

When I first started cooking, I was captivated by intricate recipes, complicated techniques, and dishes that seemed to showcase my skills in the most impressive way possible. However, over time, I've come to realize that the most memorable and flavorful dishes are often the simplest. It's easy to fall into the trap of overcomplicating things, thinking that more ingredients or more steps will automatically lead to better food. But the truth is, simplicity—when done right—is the most powerful tool in the kitchen.

Simplicity in Ingredients: Some of the most delicious dishes I've ever created were made from the humblest of ingredients: fresh tomatoes, basil, garlic, and olive oil come together in a classic pasta sauce, while a perfectly seared piece of meat needs only a little salt, pepper, and some butter. It's not about the number of ingredients you use but how you handle them. A few high-quality, fresh ingredients, prepared with care, can create something magical. This lesson applies not just to cooking but to life: sometimes, less is more, and it's the basics that form the foundation of everything great.

Story:
I remember once making a tomato sauce for a pasta dish. I was working with some of the finest tomatoes I'd ever tasted, but I was eager to complicate the recipe with too many herbs and spices. After a few attempts, I decided to strip the sauce back to its roots—just

tomatoes, garlic, olive oil, and a little salt. When I tasted it, I couldn't believe how much more vibrant the flavors were. That was a turning point in my cooking journey, a reminder that true flavor comes from honoring the simplicity of great ingredients.

---

2. The Importance of Patience: The Slow Food Movement

One of the most valuable lessons I've learned in the kitchen is the importance of patience. In our fast-paced world, there's often a rush to complete tasks and get things done quickly, but cooking—at least the kind of cooking I aspire to—takes time. Whether it's slow-roasting a piece of meat, letting a dough rise, or braising a stew for hours, the process of allowing flavors to develop and ingredients to meld is where the magic happens.

Patience is especially important in understanding the science behind cooking. For example, slow cooking not only allows flavors to become more concentrated, but it also breaks down the connective tissues in meats, making them more tender. Baking, too, is a process that requires precision and patience, from allowing dough to rise properly to letting a cake cool before slicing. By embracing the slow pace, I've learned to respect the process—and trust that the best results come with time.

The Slow Food Movement: The Slow Food movement, which emphasizes eating locally, seasonally, and sustainably, also embodies this idea of patience. It encourages us to take the time to prepare meals with intention, to appreciate the journey of making food, and to savor every moment of it.

Story:
Early in my career, I was tasked with cooking a rack of lamb for a special event. I was young and eager, and in my haste, I tried to speed up the process by cranking up the heat. The result was a tough, overcooked lamb that didn't showcase the delicate flavors I was hoping for. A mentor took me aside and explained the importance of letting the lamb cook slowly at a lower temperature, allowing the flavors to develop over time. That lesson stayed with me. The patience I learned that day has been a cornerstone of my approach to cooking ever since.

---

3. The Role of Intuition: Cooking from the Heart

While recipes are a wonderful guide, some of the best meals come when you trust your instincts. In the kitchen, intuition is developed through experience, practice, and an understanding of flavors and textures. With time, you begin to recognize what combinations work and when something feels off. Cooking from the heart means being able to listen to your ingredients, to adjust seasonings, and to have the confidence to improvise.

Understanding Your Palate: Each of us has a unique palate, shaped by our experiences and cultural background. As a chef, one of the most valuable lessons is learning how to fine-tune your palate, recognizing when a dish needs more acid, sweetness, or salt, and knowing when to stop. There's a moment in every dish where you'll know, instinctively, that it's ready. It's this connection to your food that elevates a dish from merely "good" to extraordinary.

Story:
I once prepared a soup for a family dinner—my grandmother's old recipe. The soup was hearty and comforting, but something was missing. I tasted it and felt the dish lacked a certain brightness. Without thinking too much, I squeezed in some fresh lemon juice. The moment I tasted it again, everything clicked into place. The dish came alive. That moment was a powerful reminder of how cooking is a deeply personal and intuitive process— sometimes, it's not about following a recipe, but rather responding to what the dish needs.

4. Embracing Creativity and Experimentation

Cooking is a creative expression, and in many ways, the kitchen is my canvas. While there are foundational techniques and classic dishes, the beauty of cooking lies in its infinite possibilities. Experimenting with flavors, textures, and presentation can lead to unexpected and delightful results. As I've matured as a chef, I've learned that experimentation is not just about changing the ingredients in a dish, but about understanding how those ingredients work together.

The Importance of Play: As chefs, we often focus on precision, technique, and perfection. But what I've learned is that some of the best discoveries come when we give ourselves permission to play. Whether it's trying an unusual spice or pairing unexpected flavors, allowing ourselves to break free from tradition can lead to breakthroughs. Cooking is about creativity, and creativity thrives when we embrace it without fear of failure.

Story:
Years ago, I was experimenting with a new dessert recipe for a holiday menu—chocolate and olive oil cake. The recipe called for dark chocolate, but I had an extra batch of milk chocolate on hand. In the spirit of experimentation, I decided to use the milk chocolate, which turned out to be a delicious and unexpected twist on the classic dessert. That cake became a fan favorite and a staple on the menu. This experience reinforced the idea that creativity in the kitchen can lead to the best results, often in the most unexpected ways.

5. The Connection Between Food and Memory: The Power of Food to Tell a Story

Food has an incredible power to connect us to our past, our cultures, and our memories. Some of the most powerful dishes I've created have been those that evoke a sense of nostalgia or honor a cultural tradition. Cooking is a way of telling stories. It's a way of honoring our roots, passing on family traditions, and sharing love. Each ingredient carries with it the story of a place, a moment in time, and a person.

Food as a Storytelling Tool: When I cook, I'm not just preparing a meal—I'm often telling a story. This is why certain foods, like a hearty bowl of soup or a freshly baked loaf of bread, have the power to transport us to another place or time. In my experience, cooking isn't just about creating something delicious—it's about honoring tradition, culture, and memory.

Story:
One of the most profound moments in my career came when I made my grandmother's famous apple pie for a cooking class. The students were unfamiliar with the recipe, but as soon as they tasted the pie, they were transported to their own childhoods, sharing stories of their family kitchens. That experience reminded me that food is more than just sustenance; it is a way of connecting with others, preserving history, and passing on love.

---

6. The Ever-Expanding Journey: Never Stop Learning

Culinary mastery isn't a destination; it's a lifelong journey. The beauty of cooking is that you never reach a point where there is nothing left to learn. Whether it's a new technique, a different cuisine, or a new ingredient, there's always something exciting to explore. As I reflect on my journey, I realize that each experience—whether positive or negative—has shaped me into the chef I am today.

The Joy of Exploration: Over the years, I've had the privilege of traveling, tasting, and learning from countless chefs and home cooks alike. Every meal shared, every new culture experienced, has inspired me in profound ways. The key takeaway is that there's no such thing as a "final answer" in cooking. It's a field that encourages exploration and personal expression.

Story:
One of my most memorable culinary experiences took place in Thailand, where I spent weeks learning from local chefs and home cooks. The flavors, techniques, and ingredients were so different from what I knew, but the experience deepened my appreciation for

food's ability to bridge cultures. I came back with new inspiration and techniques that transformed my cooking and opened my eyes to the endless possibilities of culinary exploration.

Conclusion:

As I reflect on my culinary journey, I realize that the lessons I've learned in the kitchen transcend cooking itself. Patience, intuition, creativity, and connection—these are qualities that we can apply to every area of our lives. Cooking is a way of expressing our love, our culture, and our personal stories. It's a journey that is always evolving, and as long as we remain open to new experiences and willing to learn, the kitchen will always be a place of discovery, creativity, and connection.

So, as you continue your own culinary adventure, remember that it's not just about the recipes—it's about the process, the people you share meals with, and the stories you tell along the way. Bon appétit!

Made in the USA
Las Vegas, NV
27 November 2024

12741948R00111